Maps and map games

Deborah Manley and Pamela Cotterill

cover illustration by David Pryle text illustrations by Ray Martin

Maps & map games

Piccolo Original
Pan Books London and Sydney

First published 1976 by Pan Books Ltd,
Cavaye Place, London SW10 9PG
3rd printing 1977
© Deborah Manley and Pamela Cotterill 1976
ISBN 0 330 24479 5
Printed and bound in Great Britain by
Cox & Wyman Ltd, London, Reading and Fakenham

Contents

Authors' note

In spring 1974 the new maps produced by the British Ordnance Survey began to go metric. At first, only the southern half of the British Isles south of a line between Morecambe in the west and Bridlington in the east was changed. The one-inch maps are the first to be affected. These have been enlarged photographically so that they are now on a scale of 1 : 50 000 (2 cm = 1 km) instead of 1 : 63 000. So the old 1-inch-to-the-mile maps now become (in terms of miles) about 1¼ inches to the mile. The other major change in these maps is in the labelling of the contour lines: these were at 50-foot intervals and labelled in feet at 250-foot intervals; now the same contours are labelled in metres, although the interval of 50 feet remains. Later, the Ordnance Survey will produce maps with contour lines redrawn to a metric vertical interval.

In writing this book we have chosen to use the 1-inch-to-the-mile map as our basis, partly because the new maps are not complete and will be changed when new surveys are made, and partly because the old maps will be in use for a long time to come. In any case, the principles of map-reading remain the same whatever scale is used.

Introduction

'What is a map ?' asked Rebecca.

'It's a picture of a place,' said Brett.

'Like a photograph ?' asked Rebecca.

'No, more like a drawing of what a bird sees as he flies overhead,' said Brett. 'A map tells you all sorts of different things about places.'

'What sort of things ?' asked Rebecca.

'Oh, things like how high the hills are and where the roads go to,' said Brett.

'What do people use maps for ?' asked Rebecca.

'So they can find the way to where they want to go,' said Brett.

'Can you find your way with a map ?' asked Rebecca.

'Well, I'm not too sure. But we could learn how to use a map, couldn't we ?' said Brett.

'That would be fun !' said Rebecca.

And so they did learn how to use a map.

And it was fun.

1 Making some maps of your own

What is a map?

A map is a drawing of an area as you would see it from high up above.

You can make maps of all sorts of places. You can make a map of your bedroom or of the world.

Making a map of things on a table
Collect together some of the following things:

1 a tin of soup   6 a saucer
2 a box of matches   7 an envelope
3 a bottle   8 a pack of cards
4 a reel of cotton   9 a pencil
5 a button   10 a leaf

Spread them out on a table or on a sheet of paper on the floor. Stand so that you can look down at them. Draw a map of what you see.

It might look like this one. Which of these pictures do you think represents which object in the list? (See **Answers**)

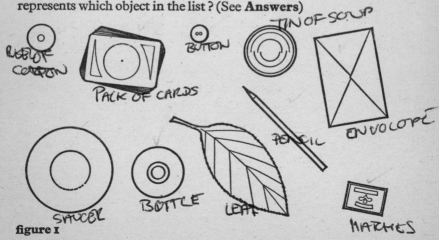

figure 1

A map of your room

Now imagine that you are a fly on the ceiling of your room. Try to draw a map of your room as the fly would see it. You couldn't get a piece of paper big enough to make all the things the same size as they really are, so you have to draw them much smaller, of course.

Figure 2 shows a picture and a map of Rebecca's room. Draw maps of other rooms in your house.

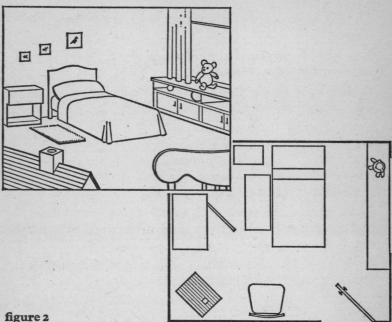

figure 2

A map of your house and garden

This time you will have to imagine that you are a bird flying over the house. Try to show on your map where the house stands in the garden. You can't show every detail, but try to show the things that you think are most important.

Figure 3 shows a picture and a map of Susannah's house and garden.

figure 3

So far none of the maps you have drawn has probably been very accurate. You can find out how to make more accurate maps later. But you can already see how a map can tell you where things are in relation to each other. Also, if you have been reasonably accurate, you have shown on your map that your house covers a greater area (that is, a larger piece of land) than, say, the garden shed. Now try to draw a map of a larger area.

A map of your neighbourhood

Imagine that a visitor asks you the way to another house near your own. Can you draw a map to show the visitor where to go ? Look at the map in **figure 4**. Tell a stranger how to get from Rebecca's house to Susannah's house on it.

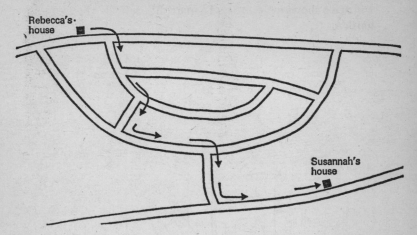

figure 4

Now draw a map of your own neighbourhood like this one. Show the roads and some of the most important landmarks.

Which is which ?

You've now made some maps of different places. Look at the two drawings and two maps in **figure 5** and see if you can say which map shows which place.

(See **Answers**)

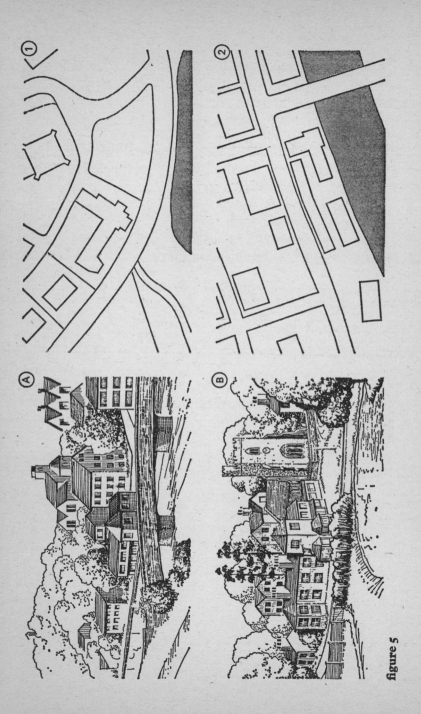

figure 5

Plans and maps

We have called all the drawings you have been making 'maps'. But really we use the word 'map' for large areas like a neighbourhood, town or piece of country. If we draw a 'map' of the inside of a house or even of a house in its garden, we usually call this sort of map a 'plan'.

Giving directions

When you tell someone how to get from one place to another, you could say that you were giving a 'word map' of the way to go.

Can you give 'word maps' of how someone would go from one place to another on the map in **figure 6**?

from the church to the school
from the butcher's shop to the cinema
from the roundabout to the station

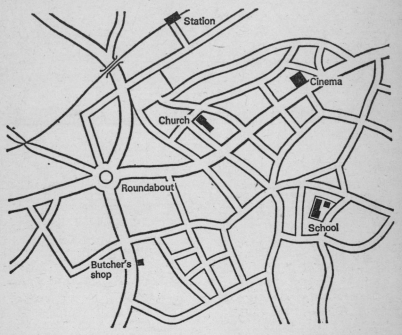

figure 6

2 How big is it? How far is it?

Even if you wanted to draw a map of a small area like your bedroom and show the objects all the same size as the real ones, you wouldn't be able to find a piece of paper large enough to draw it on. So when we draw maps, we must show the real distance and size of objects by a much smaller distance and size on paper. If you wanted to draw a map of the world, just think how small your piece of paper would be compared with the size of the world!

Scale

If you were drawing a map of your garden, you might decide to show one yard in the garden as half an inch on the map (or one metre as one centimetre). But how would someone else who looked at your map know that this is what you had decided? You would have to tell them on the map. So you could write on your map:

Scale: 1 centimetre on the map represents 1 metre
or Scale: 1 cm = 1 m
Or you could show this in a different way, as in **figure 7**.

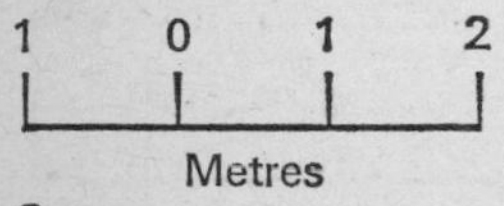

figure 7

This is called a *plain scale*.

Now anyone who looked at your map would know to what *scale* you had drawn it. They would be able to measure the distance between any two points on the map, and from this they could work out the real distance on the ground.

How far is it ?
Now look at **figure 8**. This map shows part of a town. Using
a ruler, can you tell how far it is as the crow flies
from Rebecca's house to the school ?
from Mark's house to the shop ?
from the shop to the bus stop ?
from Adam's house to Mark's house ?
How big is the school playground ?
(See **Answers**)

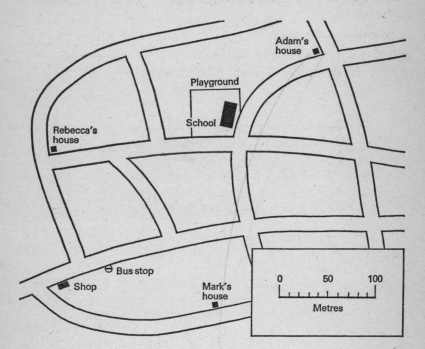

figure 8

Different scales

Of course, maps are drawn to all sorts of different scales. A map of the world might be drawn on a scale where 1 inch represents 1200 miles (or 1 centimetre represents 800 kilometres); a map of Europe or Australia in an atlas might be on a scale of 1 inch to 300 miles (or 1 centimetre to 200 kilometres); a map of Britain or New Zealand might be 1 inch to 75 miles (or 1 centimetre to 40 kilometres).

The larger the scale on a map – that is, the less distance on the ground that one inch or one centimetre represents – the more detail can be shown on it.

Look at these three maps:

In **figure 9** you can see main towns and rivers. If you put in any more detail, the map would get very confused, wouldn't it?

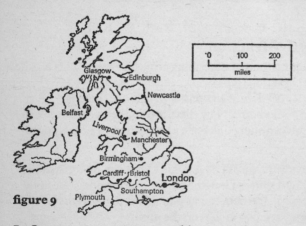

figure 9

In **figure 10** you can see roughly how large the towns are, and you can see the main roads. Notice that the length of the roads is drawn to scale; but on a map their width cannot be drawn to scale.

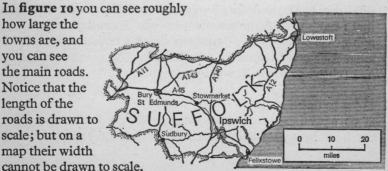

figure 10

In **figure 11** you can see the streets and open spaces.

Notice the different scales on these three maps and how, as we said, 'the larger the scale on a map, the more detail can be shown on it'.

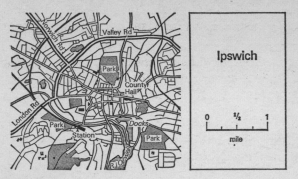

figure 11

Representative fraction

There is another method of describing scale on a map. This is called Representative Fraction (RF).

How does this work? Let us say that the scale on a map is 1 centimetre to 1 kilometre. Now there are 100 000 centimetres in a kilometre, so you can show this scale as a fraction: $\frac{1}{100\,000}$: or as 1 : 100 000.

Now, the great advantage of using RF is that it can be translated easily into different units of measurement. For instance, the scale we have just seen, 1 : 100 000, can also be taken to mean that 1 *inch* on the map shows 100 000 inches on the ground. The new maps published by the Ordnance Survey use the RF 1 : 50 000. This means that 1 centimetre on the map shows 50 000 centimetres on the ground; in other words 1 centimetre shows 500 metres, or half a kilometre; 2 centimetres show 1 kilometre. And 1 inch on these maps shows 50 000 inches on the ground.

How to use a scale

When a plain scale is drawn on a map, it is often divided up so that you can measure smaller distances on the map more easily. Look at this scale:

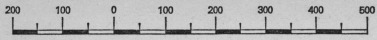

figure 12

A scale like this can be used for units of miles or of kilometres. You can measure distances of 50 or of 500 units quite easily from such a scale.

If you want to find out the distance between two points on a map, the quickest way is to place a ruler on the map and measure the distance like this:

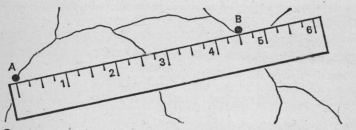

figure 13   Scale: 1 inch to 1 mile   Distance from A to B = $4\frac{1}{2}$ miles

Try this for yourself. On the map in **figure 14**, how far is it in a straight line from Appleborough to Beeton, from Beeton to Catville, from Catville to Dollhurst, and from Dollhurst to Appleborough?

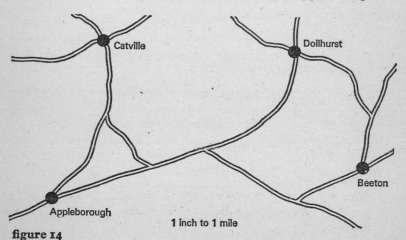

1 inch to 1 mile

figure 14

How far is it on the ground ?

But although this method shows the distance in a straight line, or 'as the crow flies', it doesn't tell you how far you might have to walk along a real road or path to get from A to B. Nor does it tell you how long a stream which winds across a stretch of land is.

To measure distances like this, take a piece of fine string and lay it on the map so that it follows the line of the path or stream. Mark the distance carefully on the string (a ball-point pen is good for this). Now measure the full length of the piece of string against a ruler.

More measuring

Now, on the map in **figure 15**, measure the distance from Coneyfield to Dancing,

1 as the crow flies
2 along the road
3 along the footpath

(See **Answers**)

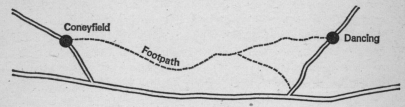

figure 15   1 inch to 1 mile

You can see that if you were planning to walk from Coneyfield to Dancing, it could be important to have measured your route and to know what the scale of your map was.

It is worth remembering that the speed at which you are travelling affects the scale of the map which you will need. If you are going by car, you will probably be travelling at about 40 miles (or 65 kilometres) an hour, so a map with a scale of 1 inch to 10 miles (or 1 centimetre to 6 kilometres) will be quite adequate to tell you all you want to know about your route. But if you are walking across country you are unlikely to be going faster than 3 miles (or about 5 kilometres) an hour, so you will need a map of about 1 inch to 1 mile (or 2 centimetres to 1 kilometre), so that you can see the details of footpaths and landmarks.

Draw your own map to scale

Now see if you can draw a map of your own garden to scale. How would you set about it ? Well, first measure the garden. You can use a yard stick or metre stick, or a tape measure; alternatively, you can pace it if you make sure that each of your paces is the same length as the others. Let us say that you are using a metre stick and that you find your garden is 20 metres long and 8 metres wide. What do you think would be a suitable scale for your map ? 10 centimetres to 1 metre would be much too big, wouldn't it ? Even 5 centimetres to 1 metre would make your map 100 centimetres long. What about a scale of 1 centimetre to 1 metre ? That would make the map 20 centimetres long and 8 centimetres wide. That would be quite a convenient size.

Now measure the other distances in the garden in paces : the size and position of the flower beds, the garden hut, the paths and the terrace. Put all these details onto your map.

Here is a map of Rebecca's garden. We have had to use a smaller scale than yours. How long is the rose bed in her garden ? How big is the garden hut ? How long is the path which goes down the garden from the house to the back fence ? What is the overall area of the lawn (remember you work out the area by multiplying the length by the width) ? (See **Answers**)

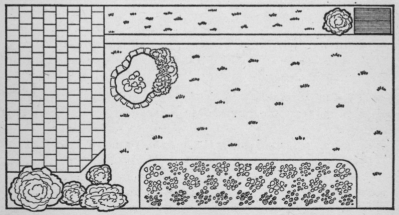

figure 16   1 inch to 20 feet

How long is a kilometre?

When we talk about drawing a map to scale and about 1 centimetre to 1 kilometre (or 1 inch to 1 mile), you know how long a centimetre is because you can look at one on a ruler, but do you really know how long a kilometre or a mile is ? You can find out for yourself.

Have you got a map of the area where you live ? Find your own street on it. Look at the scale and mark a point one kilometre from your house. Have you ever walked to that point ? If not, do so one day and then you'll know exactly what you mean when you talk about a kilometre. Do the same thing to find out how long a mile is.

3 Landmarks on maps

Map symbols

When you go for a walk in the country you see different landmarks and you walk through different kinds of country. These things can be shown on a map so that you know what you will find before you go on your walk, and so that you know your whereabouts when you reach a particular landmark. We call the signs which we use to show these things on a map *symbols*.

On most maps the symbols are made to look like very simple versions of the things which they represent. For instance, **figure 17** shows a lighthouse.

figure 17

There will probably be a *key* or list of symbols and descriptions on the map to explain to the map-reader what each symbol stands for. Sometimes actual words are used instead of pictures, and sometimes initial letters are used.

There are symbols for roads showing whether they are major or minor roads, or footpaths. There are symbols for railway lines. There are symbols for marshy ground, and for rivers and pools. There are symbols for landmarks like a windmill or a church.

The purpose of an important building is often shown on a map with initial letters or an abbreviation. P stands for post office; T for telephone; *Sch* for school; *Hosp* for hospital; *PH* for public house.

On maps which use colour, red, yellow, blue and green are also used to distinguish the different symbols. Woods are green; water is blue; main roads are often red; a red triangle is the symbol for a Youth Hostel.

Guess the meaning
The meanings of most map symbols can be guessed by using your common sense. See if you can guess what the symbols in **figure 18** stand for now, but when you are using a real map always look at the symbol key.
(Check your guesses against the **Answers**)

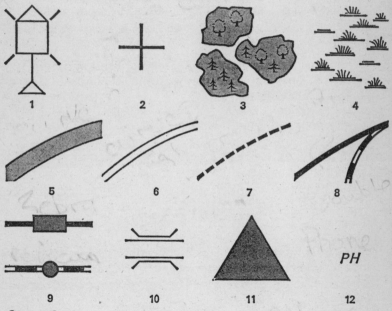

figure 18

There are more symbols in **figure 88** on page 101.

What did they see?
We are going to describe to you the walk that Rebecca and Brett took one afternoon. You trace their journey on the map in **figure 19**.

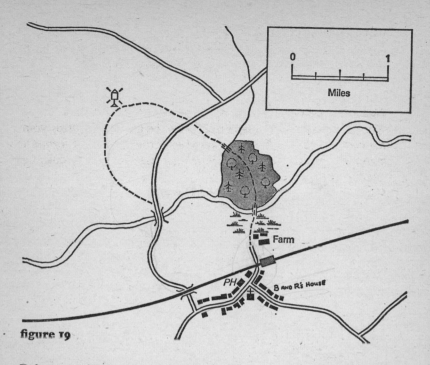

0   1

figure 19

Rebecca and Brett went past the church and out of the village. They decided to take the short cut across a field to the place where the road passes under the railway line. 'We'll save almost half a mile if we go that way,' said Brett.

For the next mile they had to walk along the road until they came to the river. About 200 yards from the bridge they turned left onto a footpath which led to a windmill. From there the footpath led back to the road, almost a mile from where they had left it. They crossed the road and walked about half a mile to the stream which went on to join the bigger river they had crossed earlier. The next three-quarters of a mile of their journey was through a wood of mixed trees.

Still keeping on the footpath, they crossed the river again, and then had to go through a patch of marshy ground. They went across the field to Holt Farm, rejoining the road just behind the station to go back into the village. They had walked the best part of six miles that day – about ten kilometres.

The make-a-map game
This is a game that you can play either on your own or with a friend.
You will need to make some equipment first.
The board:
On a sheet of paper or card draw a grid like **figure 20**, with six
numbered squares across and six numbered squares down. The
lines of the grid should be about 1 inch (or 2 centimetres) apart.
Make one grid for each person playing.

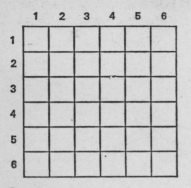

figure 20

The instruction-givers:
You will need two dice, or you can use two six-sided spinners
similar to the one shown on page 63. You will need 36 small cards
or pieces of paper. On each of 18 of the cards, draw a map symbol
(use the diagrams on page 101 as a guide). Here is a list of what you
should draw on the cards:

one of each

windmill	telephone
church	farm
public house	station
youth hostel	bridge
post office	school

two of each

evergreen wood	mixed wood
deciduous wood	marsh

Leave the other 18 cards blank.

Mix the cards up and place them face downwards on the table.

How to play:
We give an example in brackets of what could happen in one player's turn.
1 Throw one dice or spin one spinner (6)
2 Throw or spin the other (2)
3 Pick up one card (church)
4 Now record this information on your map grid. Draw in the symbol for a church on square 6 across, 2 down, as in **figure 21**.

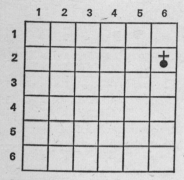

figure 21

5 Continue to throw for symbols and positions and enter them on your map grid until you have turned over all the symbol cards. As half of these are blank at least half your squares will be blank if you are playing alone, more if you are playing with a friend. Some squares may have more than one symbol on them.
6 Now complete your 'map' by drawing in the symbols for roads, footpaths, streams and railway lines. Remember that there should be an access road to most of the buildings – although there might be a footpath to the youth hostel and to the church. Remember that a road is not likely to go through a marsh, but that a stream is.
7 Add a scale to your complete map, and colour the symbols if you wish.

Battlefield

Have you ever played the game called Battleships ? This game is based on that one, but represents a land battle in which one player is trying to capture the strategic strongholds of his opponent.

The board:

Prepare two lettered and numbered grids like **figure 22.**

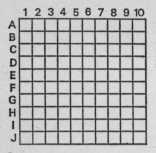

figure 22

Each player – very secretly so that his opponent can't see – marks in the following symbols for strongholds on one of his grids:

1 farmhouse (1 square)

1 windmill (1 square)

1 telephone (1 square)

1 evergreen wood (2 squares)

1 mixed wood (2 squares)

2 castles (1 of 2 squares, the other of 1 square)

1 lake (3 squares)

1 watchtower (1 square)

1 marsh (2 squares)

No two symbols (unless they are for the same object – the marsh, for example) should be in adjoining horizontal, vertical or diagonal squares.

Your grid might now look like **figure 23.**

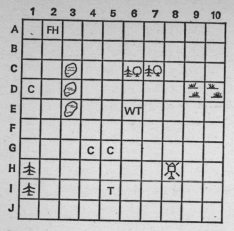

figure 23

How to play:
Remember always to sit so that your battlefield is hidden from your opponent.

1 Take it in turns to call out the name of a grid square, like A 10, J 2, B 7 and so on.

2 The other player looks at this square on his battlefield. If there is no symbol on it he says 'Miss', and you put an o in that square on your blank grid. If there is a symbol he replies 'Hit' and tells you what it is you have hit. You then mark that symbol on your blank grid.

3 When you have scored a hit, you get another turn.

4 When you have captured the whole of one of your opponent's strongholds, he says 'Captured'. Then you can cross off the squares all around the stronghold captured, since you know two symbols can't be next to each other. For instance, if you have hit a farmhouse on square B 8, you can cross off all the squares which touch it, as in **figure 24**.

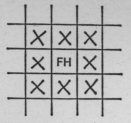

figure 24

5 The game is won when one player has captured all the strongholds on his opponent's battlefield. The loser admits defeat by saying 'Surrender'.

Country walk
This game can be played by two or more players.
Preparation:
You need to copy the board in **figure 25** onto a larger piece of paper or card. You need a counter for each player. You need twenty cards with *two* of the following symbols on each of them.

youth hostel	post office	evergreen wood
public house	windmill	marsh
telephone	mixed wood	bridge
farmhouse	deciduous wood	church
school		

Finish	☒			⁂			▲	
		⋈		Sch		♣♀		
	PO		PH		♀		T	
		♣		♀		♣♀		FH
	Sch		▲			☒		⋈
	PO			♀			PH	
			♀			⁂		
Start →		♣		T			FH	

figure 25

32

How to play:

1 Lay the cards face downwards on the table.

2 Each player takes it in turn to draw a card from this pile. He moves his counter to the nearest of the two card symbols on the board. If there is no example of that symbol ahead of him, he has to move his counter backwards to the nearest example. Then he puts his card face upwards beside the pile of cards.

3 When all the cards in the pile have been turned over, if the game is not complete, turn the pack face down and start again.

4 The first player to reach the final windmill is the winner.

4 Hills on paper

Maps are drawn on paper, which is flat, but of course everything isn't flat. There are hills and valleys, high land and low land. How can we represent all this on a piece of paper?

The ancient mapmaker, or *cartographer*, faced a formidable task when he wanted to show on his flat, two-dimensional map the shape of the land (that is, the *relief*) and the different heights of the land.

In some very old maps they simply drew the features like a landscape. A range of mountains might be shown like this:

figure 26

But although this made a nice picture, and at least told you that there *was* a range of mountains in the area, it gave no accurate idea of their shape or height or exactly where the peaks or valleys were.

As mapmaking became more sophisticated, *hachures* (pronounced 'hashures') were used to give a more accurate picture. These showed how steep the slopes were by lines drawn from high to low ground, as in **figure 27**.

figure 27

But it was still not possible to tell how high various features were, except where special points or *spot-heights* were marked on the map (see page 41).

Layer-tinting

One way of showing height is to colour the different levels of an area in different colours, as is done in many atlases. The lowest land is usually coloured green, higher land is brown (and sometimes yellow), and really high land is grey and sometimes white. A map coloured in this way is called a *physical* map because it shows the physical appearance of the land. On a physical map there will be a *key* like this, which tells you what the different colours mean:

feet		metres
12 000	grey	4 000
6 000	grey-brown	2 000
3 000	brown	1 000
1 000	brown-green	350
500	green-brown	150
0	green	0 sea level
	blue	

This key shows the height of that land above sea level, and when you look at the map you can get a very quick idea of where the highlands and lowlands are and of where there might be mountains.

We call this way of showing height layer-tinting because we tint the different layers of height in different colours.

Layer-tint this map

If you trace the map in **figure 28** onto a piece of paper, and colour the areas like this:

1 = green, 2 = brown, 3 = grey, you will have made a very simple physical map, showing the height of land in this imaginary place.

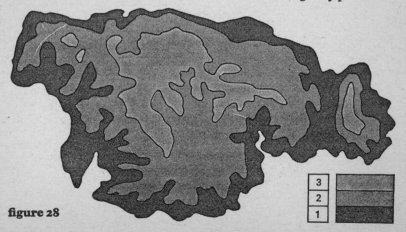

figure 28

How the problem was solved: contours

You can understand that neither layer-tinting nor hachures really
solved the problem of how to show on paper the height of the land
to an ordinary person who wanted to walk or drive across a piece of
country. The problem of showing relief on a flat piece of paper was
solved by the invention of *contour lines*. No one quite knows who
invented this method, but it is thought to have been adapted from
the method used on *charts*, or maps of the sea, to show the depth of
water around coasts.

A contour line is an imaginary line which joins all the points on the
ground that are at the same height above sea level. With contour
lines you can show the shape of hills very accurately. You will
understand more about contour lines if you make some for yourself
in the following way.

Make your own contour map
You will need a really large, rough-shaped rock. Try to find one
which has peaks and hollows and is irregularly shaped. You will also
need a big bucket or wash-basin. (An old-fashioned zinc bath or
wash-tub would be ideal.) You will need a piece of chalk, and water
to fill the bath with.

Put your rock in the middle of the bath. Pour some water round it
so your rock is like an island in the sea. All contour lines are
measured from sea level. Draw a line round your rock where the
water comes to. This line represents sea level.

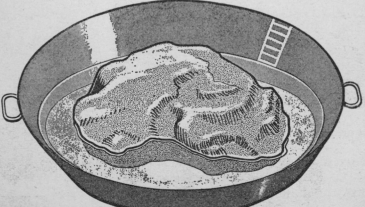

figure 29

On the inside of the bath draw a scale as in **figure 29** to show, say, 1 inch to 100 feet. (It could show 1 centimetre to 10 metres.) Now look at your rock island from immediately above, and, on a piece of paper, draw the part of the island which shows above sea level. The rock in our picture would look like **figure 30**.

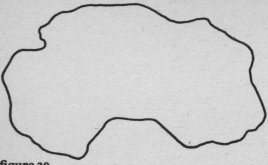

figure 30

Now pour more water into the bath so it reaches the first inch (or centimetre) measure. Draw a line round your rock again. If you are using the inch measure, this is your first contour line at 100 feet above sea level (or, if you are using the centimetre measure, this is your first contour line at 10 metres). Look down at your rock island again, and draw this line inside the sea-level line.

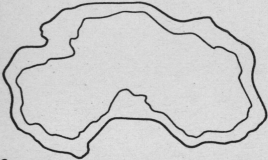

figure 31

Go on adding water inch by inch and drawing what you see. When you have finished and look down on your rock island you will be able to see the lines you have drawn on your piece of paper. Each point on each line is the same height above 'sea level' isn't it ? On your paper you have shown these contour lines. Each one represents 100 feet (or approximately 10 metres) of height, doesn't it ? So you can write in these heights on the contour map of your rock island, as in **figure 32**. (The figure for the height of each contour line is usually written in a gap in the contour line.)

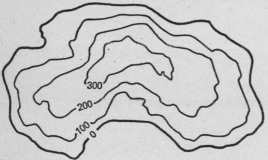

figure 32

Contour lines on a map

By looking at the contour lines on a map you can tell whether the country the map shows is flat or hilly. You can also tell how steep the hills are, for the closer together the contour lines are, the steeper the hill is. Where there is a cliff, the contour lines actually touch. Of course, a large-scale map can show you more detailed changes in height than a small-scale map.

Some interesting hill shapes

Now let us look at some individual landscape features, as shown by contours. You will find that you will learn these basic shapes very quickly and, once learned, you will quickly recognize variations of them. When you can interpret contour lines, browsing over a map can be as absorbing as reading a detective story.

The basic feature shown by contours is *slope*: widely spaced contours indicate gentle slopes; steep slopes have contours very close together; and cliffs are shown by contours running into each other.

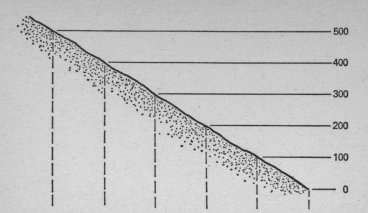

| 500
| 400
| 300
| 200
| 100
| 0

figure 33 an even slope (contour lines are evenly spaced)

figure 34 is a conical hill. But a hill that appears conical on the ground may look different on a map. For instance, **figure 35** (right) is a contour map of a ridge, but viewed end-on from north or south, it would appear like a conical hill.

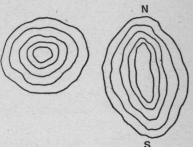

N

S

figure 36 is a range of hills with three peaks

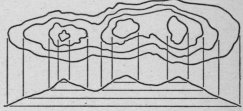

figure 37 is a *col*, or saddle – the low point between two peaks

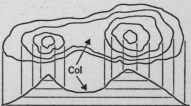

Col

figure 38 is a *pass* – the lowest point between two mountains or ranges of hills. A pass often has a river and a road – and perhaps a village – in it.

Spot-heights

We mentioned spot-heights earlier when we were talking about how mountains used to be illustrated by hachures. On a map which uses contour lines (such as an Ordnance Survey one), as well as the contour lines being labelled in feet or metres, spot-heights are marked to show particular spots like the top of a hill. These are black dots with the height in feet or metres printed alongside (see '263' in **figure 39**). These heights have been accurately measured by surveyors. Height can also be shown by *triangulation stations* which are concrete pillars built at the time of the survey; there's one on the right in **figure 39**.

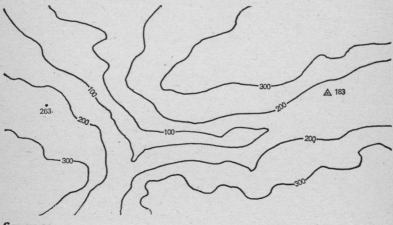

figure 39

Test yourself

1 Match the contours in **figure 40** with the description

A has steep northern slopes
B has steep western slopes
C is a perfectly conical hill
D has two summits, the western one higher
E has two summits, the southern one higher

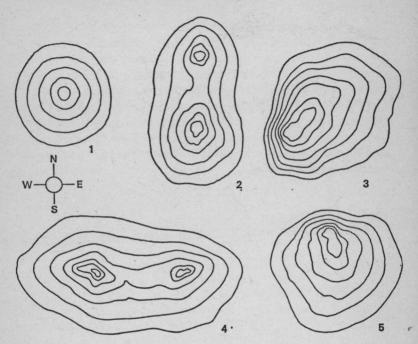

figure 40

2 Match the contour maps on the right with the shapes on the left in **figure 41**.

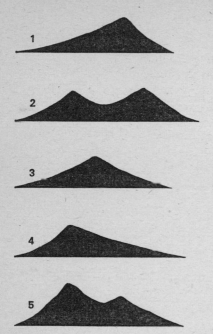

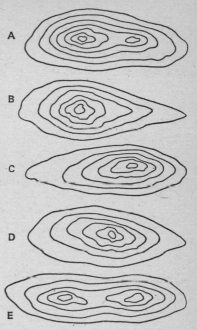

figure 41

(See **Answers**)

Making a contour model

You will need some sheets of thick, corrugated cardboard, sharp, strong scissors, glue, papier mâché, tracing paper, pots of paint, and brushes.

First, draw your own contour map. Make it large and simple, as in **figure 42**.

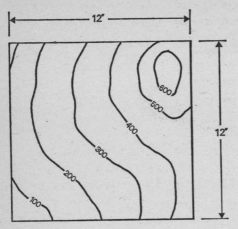

figure 42

Trace each contour onto a piece of tracing paper the same size as your map. Cut along each drawn contour line. For the map above you will have six sheets of tracing paper as in **figure 43**.

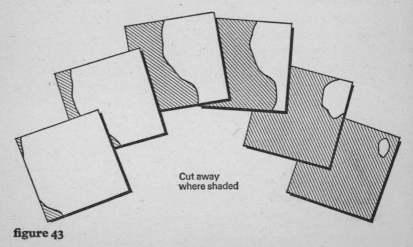

Cut away
where shaded

figure 43

Now cut enough cardboard sheets for all the contours. Decide whether you are going to use one or two pieces of cardboard for each vertical interval: I used two so that I could make a taller model. Stick the sheets of tracing paper onto the cardboard and cut the cardboard in the same way as you cut the tracing paper. Now place the lowest contour at the bottom; stick the next contour down onto it, and continue in this way until you have completed the model. Your model will look like **figure 44**.

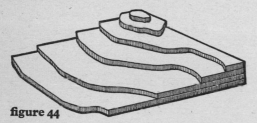

figure 44

You can fill in the 'steps' with papier mâché to give more gradual and realistic slopes. Now paint your model in different colours for each layer, from green shades to brown shades. Blobs of cottonwool dipped into green paint and stuck onto broken-off matchsticks or cocktail sticks can be added for trees. You can paint in rivers and roads in blue and brown or black. Make houses from small boxes, cut-up matchboxes and so on.

Gradients

You have now seen how you can look at a contour map and know whether you will have a steep climb or a gentle one. The amount of *slope* is known as the *gradient*.

Perhaps you have been driving in hilly country and you have seen a road sign like **figure 45**.

figure 45

This sign warns drivers that they are coming to a very steep slope on which the ground rises one foot for each ten feet travelled forwards (or, of course, one metre for every ten metres you travel forwards). When the triangle is sloping down to the right, the slope is downhill.

It is quite interesting to know what various gradients would look like if you could see them from the side:

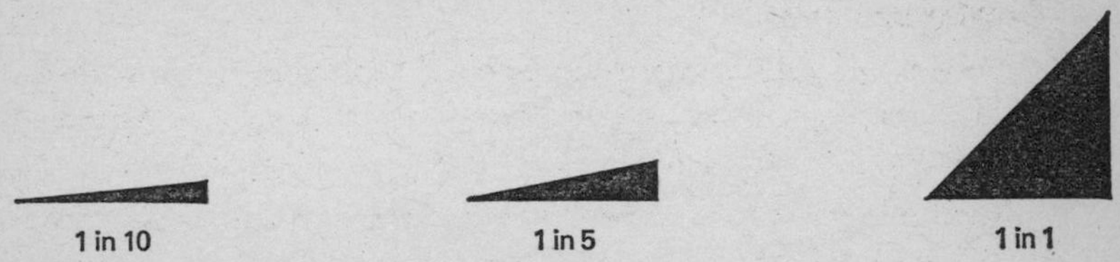

1 in 10   1 in 5   1 in 1

figure 46

Most cars will not go up a gradient of more than 1 in 4, and will only go up that in low gear. A gradient of 1 in 3 is a fairly hard climb for a walker, and a gradient of 1 in 1 is really steep and looks almost straight up when you face it. But a gradient of 1 in 1 is not, of course, vertical like a cliff face, for you are still going forward one foot for each foot that you climb upwards.

Gradients of more than 1 in 7 are marked on Ordnance Survey maps like this:

1 in 7
to 1 in 5

1 in 5
or steeper

figure 47

5 Walking with a map

Getting ready

Once you've really begun to understand how to use a map, you'll want to get out and use one. But before you do this, you do need to learn some other things.

You need to know how to get ready for hiking. You need to know how to walk safely both for your own sake and for the sake of the people who live in the places you walk through.

You'll certainly enjoy hiking more if you prepare yourself properly – have the right clothes and the right equipment and, perhaps most important, the right feet!

Preparing your feet

How do you get the right feet ? Well, make sure you have a pair of good, strong leather boots or shoes. Gym shoes and sandals are uncomfortable on long walks. And don't go out in brand-new shoes – wear them around a bit so that your feet get used to them and the leather grows suppler. Try to wear thick woollen socks. They're not always easy to buy nowadays, but at least try to get a wool mixture. And make sure that they fit. Socks which ruck up inside your shoes or slip down at the heels are a misery and socks that are too small are just as likely as shoes to give you blisters. Then, for a few days before your first major hike, wipe your soles and heels night and morning with a bit of cotton wool soaked in surgical spirit or methylated spirit. This helps to harden the skin and protects you against blisters.

The right clothes

For the rest of your clothes, wear something light but preferably windproof and showerproof – a light anorak is better than a thick sweater if it comes on to rain.

Making a map-board

When you are out doing map-work in the field it is very useful to have a map-board which acts as a desk in the open air. You need:

A sheet of heavy card or thin wood like plywood or hardboard about 10 × 12 in (or 25 × 30 cm)

One large or two smaller bulldog clips

A sheet of polythene 10 × 12 in (or 25 × 30 cm)

A pencil

A big, strong rubber band

12 in (30 cm) string

Optional: two more sheets of polythene (If you are using card rather than wood, you may wish to weather- and wear-proof this by covering it with these two sheets of polythene.)

You make up your map-board as shown here. Fold your map to a suitable size and hold the bottom edge down with the rubber band. Tie your pencil to the bulldog clip so that it is always readily available. Use your map-board for note-taking and sketching, too.

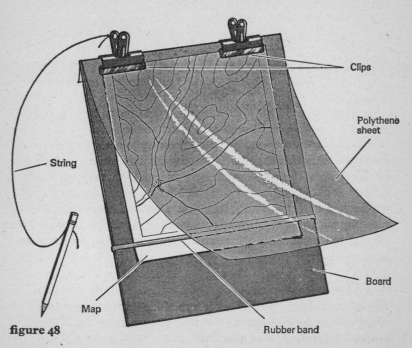

Clips

Polythene sheet

String

Board

Map

figure 48

Rubber band

Some good rules

Don't be too ambitious on your first long walk – about four miles
(or seven kilometres) would be plenty. It's better to start small and
work up to bigger things later. Remember you've got the journey
home as well as the journey out. Whatever your plans, make sure
that before you leave, you tell your family or some other responsible
person where you are going and when you would expect to be back.
It may seem unimportant, but if something goes wrong you'll be
very glad you remembered. And remember to take a map!
Wherever you walk, always remember the Country Code, which is
designed to help walkers and others to use the country without
disturbing the people and animals who live there.

The Country Code

If you open a gate, shut it behind you; if you find a gate open,
leave it open.
Avoid damage to hedges, fences and walls.
Keep to paths when you are crossing farmland.
Keep dogs under proper control.
Guard against all risk of fire.
Don't leave any litter behind you.
Safeguard water supplies.
Protect wild life, plants and trees.

What this all adds up to is: *Respect the life of the countryside.*

To the hills

When you are walking in hilly or moorland country there are
further rules which you should know for your own safety.
When you are hiking you should take reasonable precautions to
ensure your safety; but be doubly careful in wilder regions – the
mountains and the moors. Weather conditions can change without
warning. A thick mist can whoosh down on you out of the blue, and
in some areas of land without many tracks (like the Pennines, or the
Cairngorms in Scotland), you could wander around lost for days.
The shirt or blouse that was almost too hot for you in the sunny
valley will not be warm enough on the mountaintops. The
temperature drops as you go higher, and if you were caught in a

sudden damp mist you could be seriously chilled, or even suffer from exposure if you had no extra clothing to put on. In winter, especially, conditions on the British hills can become arctic.

But this is not meant to put you off going to the mountains. Indeed, in the mountains you can use your map- and compass-reading skills to the limit, and such rewards as beautiful views more than make up for the extra precautions you need to take.

Obviously, when you are climbing, you don't want to carry too much. Some foods are bulky and heavy and don't supply much energy. Good food for mountain trips is dried fruit, chocolate, barley sugar, mint cake and glucose tablets.

The Mountain Safety Code

Always travel with at least one experienced friend.

Always take a large-scale map and a compass with you, and *know how to use them*.

Wear windproof and waterproof clothes. Wear boots, not shoes. Carry gloves and spare warm clothes.

Always take food, a first-aid kit, a whistle and a torch for emergencies.

Check the weather forecast for the area before you set out – but remember that the weather may be different from the forecast.

Tell someone responsible about the route you plan to take. Make sure that you report back to that person on your return so that they know that you are back.

Give yourself plenty of time to cover your route, allowing for unplanned delays, for slower travelling and bad weather.

Know when to turn back. It is not brave to push on whatever happens – it is just silly. If you get into trouble it may bring danger to other people who have to go out to look for you.

A night on the mountain

If, for any reason, you are forced to spend a night in the mountains (perhaps you misjudged the time needed to get to your destination, or perhaps you're lost) the most important thing is not to panic. The first thing you should do is to get as low down the mountain as possible *before* darkness falls (a windy ridge or summit is not a comfortable place to spend an enforced night). Find some shelter; you might be lucky enough to find a ruined cottage. Failing that, shelter on the lee side of a wall or a large boulder. If there is heather around, or other thick vegetation, so much the better; it will keep some of the cold out of your rear end. Put on all your spare clothing, *underneath* any wet clothes you have on. Keep your socks and boots on and place your feet in the rucksack. If by any chance you have a very large polythene bag with you, you can get inside this, first tearing out a hole for your face – or you would *very* soon suffocate. Some mountaineers carry bags 6 feet (2 metres) long, made of very heavy polythene, for this purpose. But we are not recommending *you* to do this. We recommend that you should, through your map-reading and observance of the Mountain Code, never have to spend an unintended night on the mountains! Huddle closely together for warmth and nibble your food rations at frequent intervals. Be as cheerful as you can; sing, tell stories and jokes. If there are likely to be other people around, that is, if you are in a popular area, then you can give the *international mountain distress signal* (try it anyway). With either the whistle or the torch, or both, give six whistles or flashes a minute; then stop for a minute and repeat with six more signals per minute and so on. If your signal is picked up, then you will hear or see the answer, which is three signals per minute followed by a minute's silence. Help will soon come. But if there is no reply, settle down for the night as comfortably as you can. As soon as it is light enough you can make your way down the mountain. As soon as you can, telephone your parents/friends/the police and let them know that you are safe.

A day in the mountains

Rebecca was spending a holiday with Brett and his family. On the first morning, they got up very early, for it was a beautiful day and they didn't want to waste a minute of their precious holiday.

'We're off to the beach now, mum,' said Brett after breakfast, and putting their packed lunch and a 1-inch map of the area in a rucksack, they left the house happily. But they soon got bored searching the rock-pools for crabs and sea anemones.

'Let's go and climb those mountains,' said Rebecca, and Brett agreed that that would be more exciting.

'Those mountains' stood 1500 feet above the village; there were two rocky peaks, one a bit lower than the other. A broad, grassy spur from the summit led down almost to the village, but on its western side, the mountain was steep and precipitous. The children looked at the map and discovered that there was a track up the spur.

They found the start of the track just by a milestone and after walking along it for about three quarters of a mile they passed a farmhouse. They stopped for a while to chat to the farmer. 'You'll be going to the top then?' he asked. 'Well, just be careful. It's an easy route but it might come on to rain later and the mist is treacherous up there. Keep to the right, away from the cliffs, and watch out for the slate quarries – they're not fenced in and I've lost quite a few sheep down there. No people yet, though!'

The children laughed at the farmer's little joke and resolved to be careful. They found the climb easy but tiring. The slope was not steep (widely spaced contour lines) but they had to pass through a large area of bright green moss which was very boggy (marsh symbols), and their feet, in summer sandals, got very wet. They came to a steep bit (closely spaced contour lines), and the summit, which had until now been in view, disappeared from sight behind the curve of the slope. They were really exhausted and hot when they got to the top of the steep bit. There was a pleasant surprise – a small plateau (very widely spaced, or even absent, contour lines) with a small blue lake. Beyond lay the final easy rise to the summit. They sank onto the ground.

'Let's have a rest,' said Brett. 'We might even paddle in the lake.' But they went to sleep instead.

While Brett and Rebecca are resting, we can look at their route on the map in **figure 49**. You can easily find the track they took if you follow the main road until you come to the milestone (symbol *.MS*). A dashed line represents the footpath, and the farm where they stopped is marked by a black square. The track continues up the broad, grassy spur (rounded contour lines). The track is a little indistinct in places but there is no difficulty following the spur on a

figure 49

fine day. Steep parts are shown by contour lines close together and easier slopes have widely spaced contour lines. At the point where the summit disappeared behind a bulge in the slope, the children were facing a *convex* slope. This is where there is an outward curve, steep at the lower part, with easier slopes at the top. The plateau is shown by widely spaced, irregular contour lines and the lake is marked on the map. The even contour slopes above the plateau give a regular, easy path to the summit, which is really a rocky ridge, about half a mile or a kilometre long, running north-west to south-east. (See page 60 for compass points.)

The cliffs on the mountain are on the western side, but the two children were unable to see them to their left because of a smaller spur. Look at the shape of the contour lines to the left of the children's path. They curve in and out again, with the other spur farther west blocking out the view of the cliffs.

While Brett and Rebecca were asleep, the little clouds in the north had moved farther south. Soon the undersides of the clouds were just above the top of the mountain.

The children were now at 1350 feet. At this height it was colder, but they had found the drop in temperature welcome, for the long walk had made them very hot. When the clouds came over, the temperature dropped even more, and awoke Brett and Rebecca. In front of them, to the north, the high mountains of Snowdonia were by now covered in heavy cloud.

'Oh, look, it's clouding over,' said Brett. 'We'd better go down.' But Rebecca wanted to go on to the summit, which was only about 150 feet above them.

'OK, but we'd better hurry,' said Brett, who didn't really think there would be any difficulty, but was anxious to behave responsibly. They soon reached the top and had a wide view of the sea and one or two little islands, which looked like whales basking. Below them they could also see the quarry with a few ruined houses beside it. They decided to go down to explore the houses, which were just sad, grey, stone shells. They looked down into the deep hole that men had hacked out of the mountains many years ago to get the slate to roof houses throughout the world. As the farmer had said, it was unfenced, and with the clouds beginning to swirl around them they remembered his warning.

'Oh Brett,' said Rebecca anxiously, 'I'm frightened. Which way shall we go down ? Look, it's after four and your parents will be worried.'

Brett was wondering what to do too. They couldn't see the way they'd come, and he remembered that he hadn't packed the compass. He had become quite good at reading a map and using a compass but he'd never been lost in a mist before and he'd always been with someone older on mountain walks. Rebecca was younger, so he had to think for them both.

He took out the map and together they studied it. 'We know we're at the quarry,' Brett said, 'and that that road from the quarry goes roughly north. We could take it, but it would land us right on the other side of the mountains. If we turn off left here we should be able to get down this valley – there are lots of streams we could follow down.'

So off they set, and soon they reached a narrow, level place – the col between two peaks at the head of the valley. They turned southwards (left) along a boggy sheep track with rain falling gently round them. They were cold, soaked to the skin and rather frightened.

'Oh Brett, suppose we're still here when it's dark! We might die!' Rebecca's voice was tearful.

'Don't be daft,' snapped Brett, sounding more confident than he felt. Soon the ground got steeper and steeper and then the children stopped. They couldn't see the slopes below them in the mist and they were both frightened of falling over a cliff. To their left was the sound of running water.

'A stream,' said Rebecca. 'We can follow it down; they always lead into valleys.' But as they clambered round the slope they saw it was in a very rocky gully. Brett decided not to risk it; there was no way of knowing how rocky and steep it was below.

And then Brett's senses came to their assistance. He pulled the map out again (it was now rather soggy) and studied the contour lines.

'No, we can't go straight down the valley,' he said. 'Look how close these contour lines are: they're so close that there might be little cliffs outcropping that we can't see in this mist. What we should do is go to the top of the steep bit again, and follow the contours round to the left for about two miles until we reach the easier slopes – then we can cut down into the valley.'

Rebecca looked with respect at her friend and forgot to be frightened.

It was very uncomfortable in their sandals, for in contouring the slope they were going around the hill and their feet kept slipping sideways out of their sandals. Once Brett cricked his ankle so that it was a bit sore to walk on. But they reached the easier ground, and as they came below the mist the world came back into view and they could see the road in front of them – a long way away!

At seven o'clock, seven hours after they'd started from the road, the children reached the road again, exhausted and worried at the prospect of meeting anxious, angry parents, if not the police and a mountain rescue team. What a fine start to the holiday!

Some questions
Brett and Rebecca didn't follow the Mountain Safety Code in at least five different ways. Can you name them? (Check with the code on page 50.)

They decided not to follow the streams down to the valley. Why do you think this was a good decision? (See **Answers**)

6 Which way is it? Where are you?

Orientating the map

You are up in the hills with fabulous views all around you. You take out the map to see if you can find some of the hilltops on it.

To identify the hills you *orientate* the map; that is, you turn it round so that it matches the features you see in front of you.

figure 50

First choose two or three prominent objects in the landscape (not necessarily the objects you are trying to identify) and find these on the map. A wood, a church or a pond are good examples. Put the map on the ground; then turn it round until you can trace an imaginary line from yourself through the object on the map to the feature on the landscape.

Your map is now orientated. You can identify the hills by an imaginary line from you, through the map and outwards to the landscape. You could now walk to the chosen hill using the map to trace your route and to pinpoint difficulties on the way.

Orientate this map

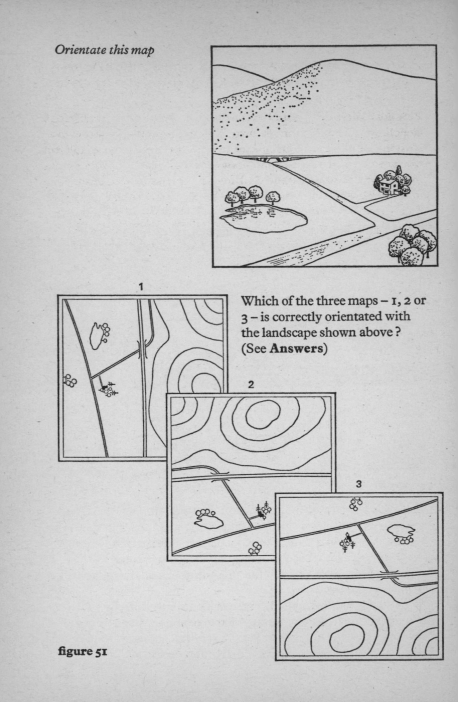

Which of the three maps – 1, 2 or 3 – is correctly orientated with the landscape shown above ? (See **Answers**)

figure 51

If you don't know where you are on the map

It may be that although you've correctly orientated the map, you don't know your own exact position on it. You can find this by a process called *lining in*.

Pick out a prominent object in the distance, let's say a church with a steeple, and identify it on the map. Then find another object *in line* with the church, but much nearer to you; say, a farmhouse. Identify the farmhouse on the map and draw a straight line from the church, through the farmhouse, and continue the line for a few inches. Now, in the same way, select two more features, at right angles to the first ones – a distant object, then a nearer one on the same line. Identify them on the map and draw a line through them. Extend the line until it meets the other one. Where the two lines meet will be your approximate position.

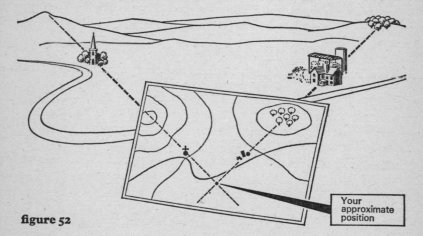

figure 52

Your approximate position

The compass points

Maps are pictures of an area which tell you where you are and how to get to a given point. But you cannot just say on an expedition, 'Go up that river for twenty miles and then turn left.' So, when we use maps, we use directions and we measure these directions with a *compass*.

You will probably know the main compass points (or *cardinal points*) already. Opposite *north* is *south* and opposite *east* is *west* (or N, S, E and W).

In between the four cardinal points are four *intermediate points*: north-west, north-east, south-west, south-east (or NW, NE, SW, and SE).

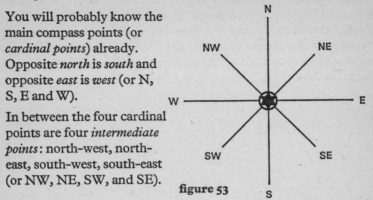

figure 53

Between these points are further subdivisions: north-north-east (which is another way of saying just east of north) and east-north-east (just north of east) and so on. You can work out the names for these subdivisions and write them in on **figure 54**.

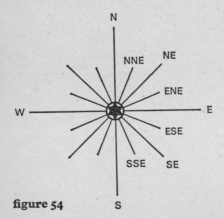

figure 54

But using these subdivisions gets a bit clumsy; and even so, it's not all that accurate. So we use the degrees of the circle to help us.

There are 360 degrees (written as 360°) in a circle. (Another way to think of this is to imagine a huge cake divided into 360 equal slices.) So between each cardinal point there are 90° (one quarter of a circle); from N to S there are 180° (half a circle) and from N to W there are 270° (three-quarters of a circle). From N to N is 360° (a full circle). You can now work out what the intermediate points are. NE is halfway between N and E, so it must be 45°. See if you can work out the correct number of degrees for the missing spaces in **figure 55**. (Check with **Answers**)

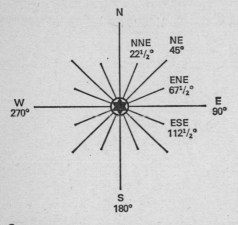

figure 55

The compasses we use for direction-finding are marked in degrees. Most of them show only 2° intervals because they are too small to show every division of the circle.

Find the wild crested dragon

Here is a game using the points of the compass.

There is a fabulous dragon hidden in these squares. He regularly eats the citizens of Nanthyranthypoo in the land of Lilipalala. No one has ever seen him except for the people he has eaten – and they had only a passing acquaintance! But, according to legend, once his likeness has been portrayed his power will die and he will wither and perish.

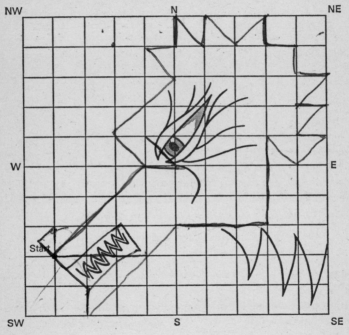

figure 56

Each side of each square represents 100 metres. Now, with a pen or pencil, follow the directions on the opposite page, drawing a line from the point START. But hurry! The people of Nanthyranthypoo are relying on you to break the dragon's power!

(All figures are given in metres. If you can't find the dragon, turn to **Answers**.)

Directions:

1	move 300 metres	NE		16	move 100 metres	E
2	100	NW		17	100	SW
3	200	NE		18	100	E
4	100	NW		19	100	SW
5	100	E		20	100	E
6	100	N		21	100	SW
7	100	SE		22	100	NW
8	100	N		23	300	S
9	100	SE		24	300	W
10	100	NE		25	300	SW
11	100	S		26	100	N
12	100	NE		27	150	NW
13	100	S		28	50	NE
14	100	E		29	150	SW
15	100	SW		30	50	NW

Let's go home

For this game you need a draughts board,
two spinners and a counter for each player.
This is how you make the spinners:
Cut two circles of card about 1½ inches
(4 cm) across.
Divide each into eight parts, like this:

figure 57

Then cut across the
points where the lines
join the edge of the
circle, so that you have
an eight-sided spinner,
like this:

figure 58

Now, write the numbers
1 to 8 in the sections of
one spinner.
On the other spinner
write the four cardinal
and four secondary
directions of a compass,
like this:

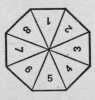

figure 59

Now put a matchstick or other short stick through the centre of each spinner, so that you can turn it like a top (see **figure 60**). The number the spinner comes to rest on is the one to count.

figure 60

The aim is to get your counters to Home. Now you are ready to play. Position your draughts board so that the top of it is towards the north from where the players are sitting, the left and right sides west and east respectively and the bottom towards the south. The nine squares in the top right-hand corner are Home. Put all your counters off the board at the south-west corner. Take it in turns to spin both counters and to move as the spinners instruct you.

Say that the first player spins 6 on the counting spinner and NE on the direction spinner. He can then move 6 points diagonally north-eastwards across the board, counting the first square as one. The players then take turns to spin and move. Some throws will take you off the board and you must miss this turn.

The winner is the first player to get his counter 'home' on one of the nine squares in the top right-hand corner.

True north

Brett and Rebecca were staring hard at the night sky.

'There it is!' said Rebecca, triumphantly pointing at the Pole Star. 'That's north.'

'Well done, Rebecca,' said Brett. 'Now, how did you find it?'

'Well, see the Plough there – those seven stars in a kind of spoon shape? Those two stars at the end are the Pointers, and if you follow them overhead they lead you to the Pole Star.'

'Very good,' said Brett approvingly. 'Now, if you walked in the direction of the Pole Star for hundreds of miles where would you arrive?'

'At the North Pole, of course,' replied Rebecca scornfully.

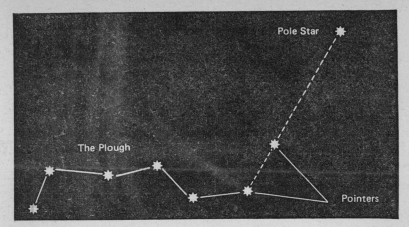

figure 61

'Everyone knows that at the North Pole, the Pole Star would be almost directly overhead.'

'You know a lot, don't you ?' Brett said admiringly. 'But did you know that there are two other norths as well ?'

'What, more ?' exclaimed Rebecca in dismay. 'I don't believe it. How can you have *three* norths ?'

While the two friends are arguing about it, we'll explain what the other norths are. First let's talk about the north Rebecca knew about: true north.

True north lies at the top axis of the Earth (the axis is an imaginary line through the centre of the Earth from top to bottom on which the Earth rotates). True south is at the bottom of the axis in Antarctica, and in the Southern Hemisphere it can be found from a constellation of stars known as the Southern Cross.

To find north by your watch
If you have the correct local time you can find true north. When it is Greenwich Mean Time (between October and March), hold your watch horizontally so that the hour hand points into the sun. Ignore the minute hand in your calculations. Take an imaginary line between the hour hand and the 12 on the watchface – this will be the approximate direction of due south. North is obviously in the opposite direction.

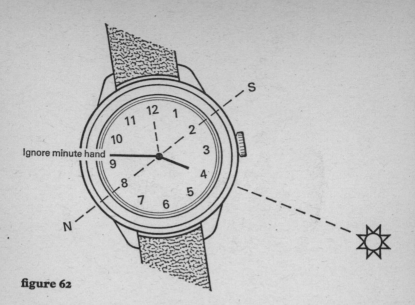

figure 62

However, when we are using British Summer Time (or if you are in a place which uses Central European Time throughout the year), you take a line between the figure 1 and the hour hand to find south. If you live in the Southern Hemisphere, you use this same method, except that the line between 12 and the hour hand actually gives you north itself.

The second north: magnetic north

The North Pole, marking true north, is at the top of the Earth's imaginary axis. Another north lies in the Hudson Bay area of Canada – this is the Earth's *magnetic* north. The Earth is like a gigantic magnet, and like an ordinary magnet, it has north and south magnetic poles. When you use a compass to find north, the south magnetic pole of the compass (usually coloured red or black) is attracted to the north magnetic pole of the Earth, and the north magnetic pole of the compass is attracted to the Earth's south magnetic pole.

The north magnetic pole is a few degrees west of true north, and because of the way the earth rotates, this difference (or *variation*) changes slightly each year. When you use a compass the needle

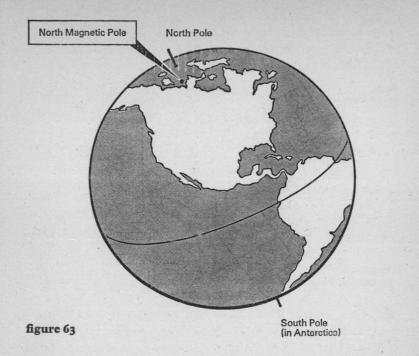

North Magnetic Pole   North Pole

figure 63

South Pole
(in Antarctica)

points to magnetic north and not to true north. We have to remember this difference when we use map and compass together.

The compass

No one really knows who discovered the principles of the compass, but the Chinese knew, about 5,000 years ago, that a piece of rock containing ore, if suspended freely, always pointed in the same direction. This direction is *magnetic north*.

The compass needle is simply a strip of magnetized metal suspended freely inside the compass casing so that it will always point to magnetic north, just like the ore-bearing rock of the Chinese. Because the needle always points to magnetic north, we can use a compass to pinpoint any direction in which we wish to travel, using the degrees of a circle.

Here is a picture of the sort of compass which is suitable for walking. It has a plastic base with inch and millimetre scales which serve as both a ruler and a protractor. This type of compass is much better than an ordinary one, especially if you are interested in orienteering – and we will be using it to explain things to you in the rest of this book.

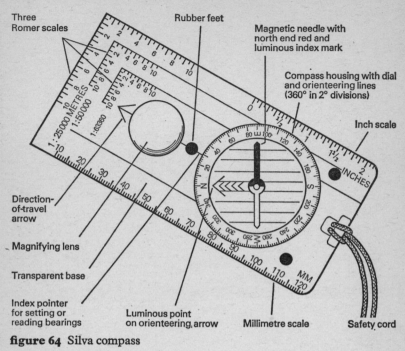

figure 64 Silva compass

Using a compass during a walk

This section may be a bit difficult to follow when you read it, so go out with a compass (like the one illustrated) and it will be much easier to understand.

Select a point in the distance to walk to – it might be a church tower, or a hill. Hold the compass horizontally with the *direction-of-travel arrow* pointing towards the object. Turn the compass round anticlockwise until the coloured end of the needle is lined up with the *orienteering arrow* (printed on the base inside). Now read off the number of degrees at the index pointer. The compass is now set.

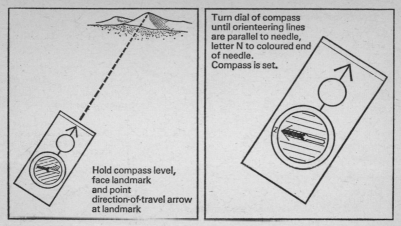

Turn dial of compass until orienteering lines are parallel to needle, letter N to coloured end of needle. Compass is set.

Hold compass level, face landmark and point direction-of-travel arrow at landmark

figure 65

Facing the bearing

Now hold the set compass flat in your hand. Turn yourself and the compass around slowly; as you change direction the compass needle will wobble violently. When you have turned so the coloured end of the needle faces the letter N (north) on the compass dial and is parallel with the *orienteering lines*, the direction-of-travel arrow on the plastic mount is pointing in the direction for you to travel.

But once you start walking on this bearing, the compass needle will begin to jump about all over the place and soon you'll be off-course. The way to follow a bearing is to sight an object near at hand, but *on the line of the bearing*. It could be a tree or a boulder. Put the compass away until you reach the tree or boulder. Then take the compass out again, check the bearing, and sight another near-by landmark on the line of travel.

While you are walking on a compass bearing you may meet an obstacle, such as a quarry, which you can hardly expect to walk through (I nearly *fell* into one many years ago when I was travelling in a mist). To get round the obstacle, set off at 90° (a quarter-circle) on the compass bearing, then walk until you reach the edge of the obstacle. *Count the number of paces you take.* Turn again at a right angle (90°) and walk forward on the original bearing until you have passed the obstacle. Then again turn through 90° and move forward

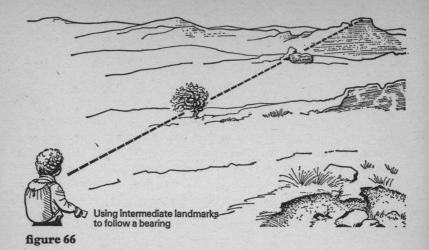

Using intermediate landmarks to follow a bearing

figure 66

the *number of paces you previously counted*. Turn finally through 90°
and you will be all set to move forward to your destination on your
compass bearing.

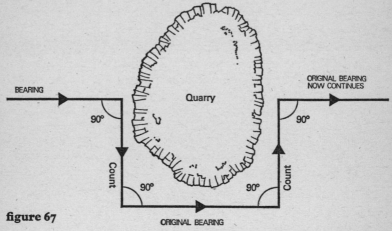

BEARING

90°

ORIGINAL BEARING
NOW CONTINUES

90°

Count

Quarry

90°

90°

Count

figure 67

ORIGINAL BEARING

Find the Coin!

This is a game which will help you to become familiar with using the compass. You need to be outside, in the garden or the park. Don't forget to take your compass with you!

Place a 10p piece at your feet. Set the compass to any bearing under 120°; say, 40°. Now face this bearing and walk 15 paces forward. Stop! Now add 120° to your bearing: 40 + 120 = 160°. Turn the dial to 160° and face the bearing. Walk 15 paces in the new direction – stop. Add another 120°: 160° + 120° = 280°. Turn the compass housing to 280°, then pace out 15 steps in the new direction. The 10p piece should be at your feet! If it isn't, then you've made a mistake somewhere. Try again until it works.

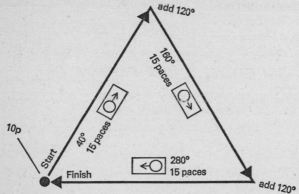

figure 68

The third north and the National Grid

Rebecca and Brett eventually sorted out the two norths, and then Brett explained about a third north – *grid north*.

If you look at any Ordnance Survey map you will see that it has printed over it a network of fine black lines running from north to south and from east to west. This is part of the National Grid System and by using the grid, any point in the country can be found on a map from a reference number.

Figure 69 shows how the whole country is covered by this network. The lines on this map are 100 kilometres apart, but if you are using the 1 : 50 000 map, your grid will have 1-kilometre squares. The vertical lines of the grid do not run exactly north-south; but unlike magnetic north, the variation from true north is so slight that we can ignore it for almost all map-reading purposes. When we take a compass bearing on the map we are taking a bearing on *grid north*.

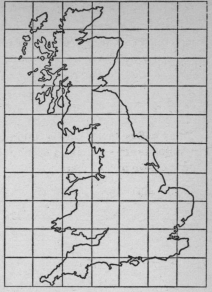

figure 69

At the bottom of the Ordnance Survey sheets is a little diagram like that in **figure 70**, which shows the degree of variation between the three norths.

figure 70

Finding a place on the National Grid

In **figure 71**, the square marked A would be indicated by the figures 75 and 22. When we give a map-reference we always first give the numbers referring to the north-south line that forms the west edge of the square. As the square referred to lies *east* of this line, this number is known as an *easting*. The next number refers to the east-west line that forms the south edge of the square. As the square lies *north* of this line, this part of the number is called the *northing*.

Don't forget this rule in giving map references: *eastings first, northings second.*

Now the figure reference we have given above is a *four-figure* reference, and refers only to the square. If we use a *six-figure* reference we can locate (to within a hundred metres) any detail within the square, for instance, the spot-height marking the mountain peak in square 75:21. To use a six-figure reference we must imagine a grid of vertical and horizontal lines over the square. There will be ten divisions running east-to-west and ten divisions running north-to-south. On the map in **figure 71**, this network has been drawn in on square 75:22.

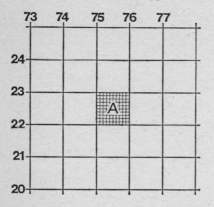

figure 71

Now we can pinpoint the position of the mountain peak. Taking the easting first (75), we estimate three tenths eastwards: this gives us a figure of 753. Now, taking the northing (21), we estimate two tenths northwards and this gives us a figure of 212. The complete six-figure reference is 753, 212, or 753212.

Romer scales

An easy way of calculating a grid reference accurately is to use a romer. Three romers are shown on the Silva compass in **figure 64** (page 68). Choose the romer scale appropriate to the scale of your map and place its zero corner on the object you are pinpointing. Now count along the top edge to find the third easting reference, and then down the vertical edge to find the third northing reference.

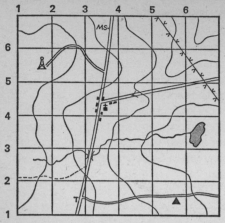

figure 72

A grid game
Here is a game to play with a dice and the grid in **figure 72**. Each player throws the dice four times and writes down each number that he throws. Use the four numbers as a four-figure grid reference and write down what you find at that point. Score one point if there is a symbol at that point; if there is nothing there, then the score is nil. The winner is the first player to reach a score of five.

Which way is it ?
Look at the map in **figure 73** and see if you can answer these questions. Try to give your answers in four-figure grid references.

At what grid reference would you:
  1 be able to buy a cool, refreshing drink
    (if you were old enough!) ?
  2 post a letter ?
  3 go apple scrumping ?
  4 cross the river ?
  5 go to Sunday-morning service ?
  6 be careful coming downhill ?
  7 explore an old ruin ?
  8 catch a bus ?
  9 get your feet wet ?
 10 cross the river by ferry ?
    (See **Answers**)

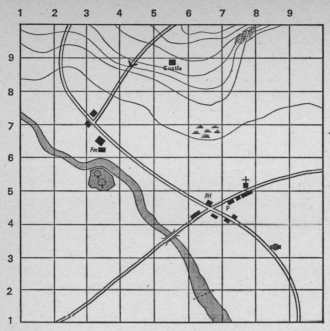

figure 73

Using a compass and map

When Rebecca understood the basic principles of the compass, Brett decided it was time to do some work with compass and map. They were spending a short holiday in the West Country in a place renowned for mist and rain. There were some nice, rugged, but not-too-dangerous hills near by, and they decided to plan a walk along these hills using their compass.

They spent Saturday night poring over the local Ordnance Survey map and eventually worked out an easy route to follow. The sketch-map in **figure 74** shows what their map looked like when they'd finished. They worked out all the compass bearings they'd need to follow and here's how they did it.

Brett first of all lined up the left edge of his compass along the line of travel for the first part of their journey, that is, from their cottage on the B3606 to the summit of the Hill of the Crow. Then he turned

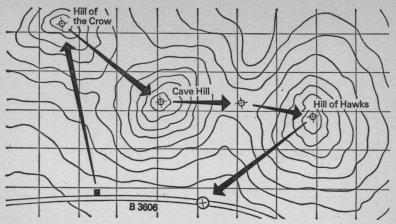

figure 74

the compass housing round until the orienteering lines were parallel with the north-south grid lines on the map.

He read off the bearing from the index pointer. It showed 348°!

'Well that's the first one done,' said Rebecca.

'Oh no, you've forgotten something,' replied Brett.

'What? Oh yes, this is a *magnetic* bearing, we must add on to convert it to a grid bearing that we can actually follow.'

'Yes,' said Brett. 'Now, how are we going to do that?'

Rebecca was helpful. 'We must find out the degree of variation between magnetic north and grid north, then add on the difference to our magnetic bearing. If we look at the bottom of the map we should find it.'

Sure enough, the information was there. For the year 1973 the variation was 8° west of grid north.

'If we followed the magnetic bearing we'd miss the summit,' said Brett, 'so now we must *add* 8° on to the magnetic bearing to turn it into a grid bearing. That makes it 356°.' As he said this he turned the compass housing round to add on the 8°. '*That's* the bearing we must follow. And look, we must remember when we set the bearing tomorrow that we must turn the whole compass round so that the needle points to north on the compass and is parallel to the orienteering lines to give us the direction of travel.'

So they planned the rest of the route in the same way and finished up with the route card shown in **figure 75**.

		APPROX.	BEARING
1.	To Hill of the Crow.	2¾ miles	348° + 8° = 356°
2.	Hill of the Crow to Cave Hill.	2 miles	128° + 8° = 136°
3.	Cave Hill to the pass.	1¼ miles	90° + 8° = 98°
4.	Pass to Hill of Hawks	1½ miles	100° + 8° = 108°
5.	Hill of Hawks to road	2¼ miles	231° + 8° = 239°

figure 75

The next day they set off on their expedition, leaving a copy of the route card with their parents – just as insurance. They were properly dressed in boots and warm clothes. They carried food and extra clothes in a rucksack, together with the map and, this time, the compass.

They had a marvellous day, and just as they were climbing up Cave Hill, a mist came down. They were delighted for this meant that they would have to travel 'blind', as it were, and could really test how accurate their compass-work had been.

Three hours later they arrived home, jubilant at their success. How different it was from the last time they'd been out in the hills!

Try it yourself
For an exercise you can check their bearings yourself on the sketch map in **figure 74**.

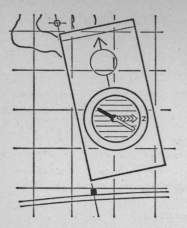

figure 76 Line up the left edge of the compass along the line of travel (cottage to summit of Hill of the Crow).

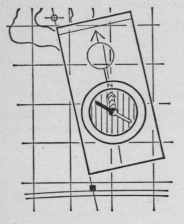

figure 77 Turn the compass housing until the orienteering lines are parallel with the grid lines of the map. Read the bearing and add on 8 ° by turning the compass housing round in anticlockwise direction.

figure 78 When you follow a bearing, allow the needle to swing round until it points to N on the compass and is parallel with the orienteering lines. Follow direction-of-travel arrow.

Don't forget that the 8° westerly variation from grid north only applies to the British Isles. In other countries it might be different; it could even be an easterly variation, in which case you would subtract instead of adding on. And just to make things more complicated, the amount of variation changes very slightly every year. At the present time it is *decreasing* by about $\frac{1}{2}$° every eight years. But if you are using a 1973 edition, or later editions of Ordnance Survey maps, you will not need to make any additional calculations until about 1980, when you would simply subtract $\frac{1}{2}$° from 8°. If you have to use a very old map which gives you the magnetic variation for, say, 1953, it would be wiser to check the current variation from an up-to-date map in your local library.

Other ways of getting your bearings

Here are some ways of finding direction which have been used for thousands of years but can still be used today.

Sunrise and sunset: the sun rises in the east and sets in the west. You can remember this with the help of this verse:
Bread rises in the yeast;
Bread sets behind the vest.
The sun rises in the east,
And sets behind the west.

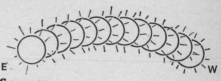

figure 79

Put a stick in the ground. The stick's shadow is shortest when the sun is due south.

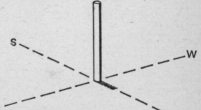

figure 80

The stump of a felled tree can give you a clue. The bark and growth rings are thicker on the north side where less sunlight has fallen on the tree while it was growing.

figure 81

Prevailing winds. Trees are shaped by the prevailing wind, especially isolated trees. The tree generally leans in the direction of the wind and short branches face the wind. In the British Isles wet south-westerlies are the most common prevailing winds.

figure 82

Observation
Using your compass where necessary, check these facts against your own observations:

The altar is usually at the east end of a church.
Moss grows better on the sheltered east or north-east sides of trees.
The sun rises in the east and sets in the west.
Trees lean away from the prevailing wind. What do you think is the prevailing wind in your area?
South winds are warm winds; east winds are cold winds.

Can you think of ways in which you might use some of this information when you were on an expedition?

Crossword quiz I

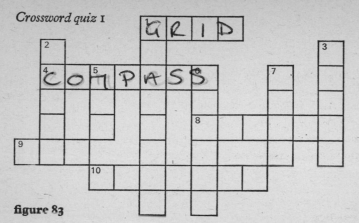

figure 83

Across
1 Squares on a map
4 Always take one with you in the mountains
8 Distance above sea level
9 Unlocks the secrets of maps
10 Imaginary line joining points of equal height

Down
1 Steepness of slope
2 Ratio of map distance to ground distance
3 There are three of these
5 Shows you where to go
6 Its abbreviation is 'Sch'
7 Symbol

(See **Answers**)

7 Orienteering: finding your way with map and compass

Navigation is not just the skill of reading a map and relating it to the landscape, nor yet being able to travel on compass bearings; it is also the ability to judge the nature of the land you will travel over and to plan a route across country. All these things are involved in the sport of *orienteering*, an outdoor pastime which is becoming more and more popular.

In the western world the majority of people live in large cities and towns and we have lost the feeling for the country which our hunting and farming ancestors had. Without special training, or tremendous luck, we would not be able to navigate a course through a wild area. But by reading a map and using a compass 'in the field', we can begin to learn this lost sense again.

Imagine your way

Intelligent and imaginative reading of a map can give you a mental picture of an unknown landscape. Contours can be 'read' as hills and mountains with spurs and valleys. In your imagination, you will be able to pick out a sensible route to your destination across country that is strange to you in reality, but which you have already pictured in your mind from reading your map – avoiding hazards such as marshy ground or slopes which will be exhausting to climb.

Orienteering as a sport

Orienteering is a fast-growing sport that involves people of all ages, from nine to ninety. It uses all the knowledge you have gained in map-reading and compass use. It really helps you to understand the map and it is also a great deal of fun. To describe it very simply: someone goes out in advance to hang up marker flags at various places, such as at a pond, an isolated tree, or a prominent boulder. These are known as 'controls'. He comes back and shows the others on the map where these flags are hung, usually by giving a grid reference. They then go off to locate all the flags, using maps and compasses and their navigational sense. Sometimes orienteering is done as a race, the winner being the person who visits all the controls and returns in the fastest time.

This book does not intend to be a complete manual of orienteering – it is best to learn the craft with other orienteers – but we do hope to let you taste some of the flavour of the game. If you feel you would like to try for yourself, then you can write to the address at the end of this section. Orienteering clubs, some with junior sections, have been started up all over the country and there may well be one near where you live. Alternatively, you might be able to persuade your geography or PE teacher at school to organize an orienteering club. Maybe the local Scouts or Guides include it as one of their outdoor activities.

An indoor orienteering game
In a large room, stick a number of coloured drawing pins at various places on the floor. Stand in the middle of the room, marking the

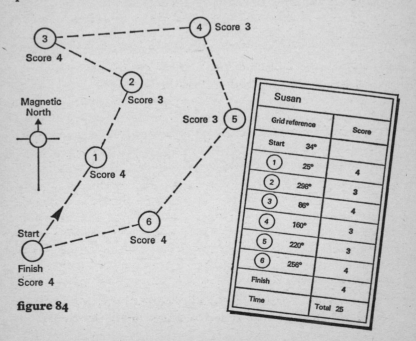

figure 84

floor so you know where START point is. With the compass, take magnetic bearings on each of the drawing pins. Now write down all the bearings and hand the list to the 'competitors'. With their compasses they set off to locate all the pins (if you can put a number on each pin so that the competitors can record the number, you will have a check that all the pins were really found!). First one to find them all is the winner.

An outdoor orienteering game

The same game can be played over an area like a small park, where there are natural objects, such as trees, the corner of a fence, a boulder, a rabbit hole and so on. You can also use tin lids placed at various points on the ground. A marker flag, made from brown paper or canvas, can be hung on or by the object or stuck into the ground on a stick. Numbers can be painted on the flags. You can give each marker flag a score value: a high number for those which are more difficult to find, and a low value for the nearer or more easily found ones. In addition, impose a time limit – say 30 minutes in a small park. The competitors note down the score numbers on bits of paper and the winner is the person with the highest score in the shortest time.

Cross-country orienteering

The most popular form of orienteering is that played across country. For this you need to be able to use your map and compass almost automatically and to choose the safest and fastest routes between the control points. But, of course, all orienteers have to begin at the beginning, and it is through orienteering with more experienced people that you learn these skills.

The course may be anything from a couple of miles to twenty in length. Control markers are placed at various points on the course and in competition orienteering, there will be an official at the control point to record the name or number of each competitor who reaches the control. Each control has a score number. The controls have to be visited in a certain order, but the choice of route between controls is left to the orienteer.

The competitors set off at intervals to visit all the controls and the person with the highest score and the fastest time is the winner.

Here is a map showing a simple cross-country orienteering route and a story about Brett and Rebecca's attempt at orienteering. While you are reading the story it is essential to refer to the map in **figure 85**. The dotted line shows their route over the course, and the story tells you about why they chose that route.

Another adventure

Once again Brett and Rebecca were excited. Today there was going to be another adventure! They scanned the sky but the few clouds rushing across it didn't seem really threatening. They were going on a cross-country orienteering race with the small school group Brett had belonged to for about a month. Miss Dobson, the geography teacher, ran the club and all members of it were very enthusiastic.

Rebecca hadn't done cross-country orienteering before, although she had done, very successfully, all the 'room' and playing-field orienteering practice with Brett, so she was particularly excited.

They dressed quickly in warm trousers and sweaters and put on strong walking shoes. They did not forget to take their compass! Then they went down to the school to meet up with the club, eight children and five teachers.

They piled into the mini-bus, and as they all chattered excitedly together they were driven about twenty miles away to a tiny village set at the foot of a range of three hills. The village was situated at the junction of three roads; houses and shops lined the roads and there was a church on the junction itself. Opposite the church they found Miss Dobson's house, which was to be the starting point for the competition. She was waiting for them with cups of tea and lemonade, and when they'd all finished drinking, the other teachers went off, for they were acting as 'officials' and would be waiting at each of the control points.

Then Miss Dobson gave each child a map of the area. The map was a black-and-white reproduction of the 1:25 000 ($2\frac{1}{2}$ inches to the mile) map of the area. She showed them the master map, which was exactly the same except that the control points had been ringed in red ink. All the children copied the circled control points onto their own maps, and then it was time for the first pair to set off. Whilst Brett and Rebecca waited for their turn they studied the map and looked at their written instructions, which looked like this:

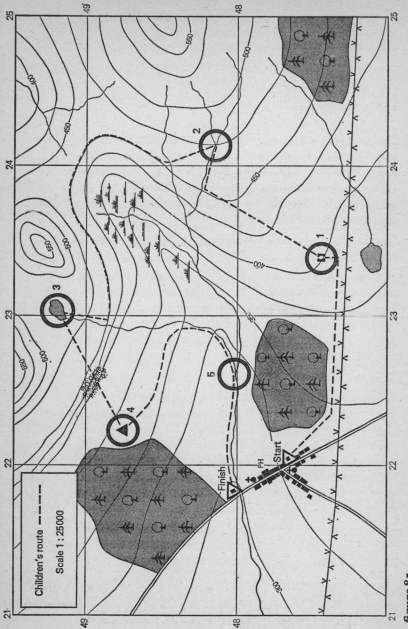

figure 85

Control	Grid reference
1 ruin	234474
2 junction of 2 streams	242482
3 small lake	230493
4 youth hostel	223488
5 junction of two streams	227480
Finish downstream to road	218480

'Are we going to take a grid bearing on the first control – the ruin ?' asked Rebecca. Brett was concentrating hard on the map. 'No, I don't think we need to,' he replied. 'See the powerline here ? It goes right past the ruin. We just need to go south-east until we reach the powerline and follow it east until we are opposite the ruin. Then we turn north to reach the ruin.'

'But suppose we can't see the ruin from the powerline ?' objected Rebecca.

'We can use the lake on the opposite side of the powerline as our guide,' replied Brett. 'It's just opposite the ruin to the south. We don't have to use grid bearings if we can use a feature of the land-scape as a kind of "handrail", which is what this powerline is. It's most important to use your wits and to be able to use anything that will help you navigate.'

'Oh,' said Rebecca.

When it was their turn to go, they set off at a good pace, not too fast. They took a compass bearing on south-east and walked in this direction over rough grassland for about a quarter of a mile. The pylons loomed up in the distance, like great striding giants from outer space. The children turned left to keep a parallel course with the powerlines up a gently sloping hillside covered with bracken. On their left was a wood and they could hear some noises from within the trees.

'Are you sure we're on the right course ?' came a disembodied voice. 'Miss Dobson would never send us through this wood – it's more like an African jungle. I'm scratched to ribbons.'

'Yes,' came the harassed answer. 'I'm sure we're on the right course, I took an absolutely accurate bearing on the ruin.'

Brett and Rebecca passed on. 'Well, we've passed Jane and Adam,' said Brett, looking a bit pleased. 'They've taken a bearing on the ruin and they're following it directly – and they've landed themselves in thick jungle! So we were wise to make this slight detour. It'll make us quicker in the end.'

They were enjoying themselves. Their pace was fairly slow and they were able to look around them as they walked. The landscape was only gently hilly, but the autumn sun made the dying bracken flame across the hills. They were now above the wood in which Jane and Adam were struggling. The golds and yellows of the deciduous trees contrasted with the sombre green of the fir trees. Soon the lake came into view, shining so brightly in the sun they couldn't look at it. They walked until they were half way along the lake. They couldn't see the ruin, but it should be opposite so they took a compass bearing on north and followed it for a few yards. Yes, there it was – an old shepherd's cottage in a copse of trees. Then they saw a red marker flag, and Miss Dwaite peered out of a window to greet them. 'Well done,' she said. 'You're doing well.'

She marked them down in her book and Brett said, 'Well, that's number one. Now for two, the junction of streams. Let's look at the map.'

They studied it carefully and thought they should take a compass bearing. Rebecca, who was beginning to get the idea, said, 'Why don't we just follow the contours round until we reach the stream, then follow the stream uphill until we reach the junction?'

'That's good,' Brett said admiringly. 'We could do that and it'd work. But look, if we go straight uphill we'll have a shorter walk. The amount of climbing on both routes is about the same – 75 feet – so it's quicker if we take the shorter route on a bearing.'

'But,' objected Rebecca, 'if we made a mistake following the compass we might miss the stream junction, and not know whether we were above it or below.'

Brett was impressed by Rebecca's logic, for this was a danger in following grid bearings. 'Well,' he replied, 'we'll "aim-off" then. We take a bearing on a point *below* the stream junction – look, around here on the 450-foot contour line – even if we make a mistake then, all we have to do is turn uphill to reach it.'

So they took a grid bearing on the map; they added 9° to the reading to convert it into a field bearing (read the story on pages 75–7 again if you've forgotten how this is done). Their field bearing was 37°.

They said goodbye to Miss Dwaite and off they went. They had to climb over a spur (curved contour lines). There was a big boulder on the skyline in their direction of travel and they used this to lead them on their course. Once past the boulder, they were on the other side of the hill overlooking a valley. They continued climbing gently, still on their bearing, this time using an isolated pine tree to follow. They passed the tree and saw the stream ahead of them. They turned right, going more steeply uphill and soon they reached the junction of streams. Mrs Smith was sitting there, eating a sandwich.

'Hello, you two,' she said. 'You're making excellent time. Are you enjoying it?' She recorded their names and gave them a piece of chocolate as they settled down to study the map again.

'Look,' said Rebecca. 'I can see Peter and Carol down there going on to three.' Number three was a small lake between the two summits on the opposite side of the valley. 'Let's follow them.'

Brett frowned. 'I don't think that's a good idea. Look at the map – there's quite a lot of marshland down there – I don't fancy getting my feet wet! See, down in the valley – you can see the marsh, those patches of bright green. Also, if we go that way, it means we have to climb down a hundred feet, then climb up another hundred feet to reach the lake.'

'So we contour then?'

'Yes,' beamed Brett. 'It's a longer route on the map but it's really shorter in time. We can descend a bit now till we're at about the 450-foot contour. Then, if we follow that contour round the head of the valley, it will take us almost to the lake. The lake's on a wide plateau with a summit sticking up on either side.'

'But we might miss the lake,' said Rebecca. 'Shouldn't we follow the contour round until we reach the stream that flows from the lake, then we can turn and follow it up to the lake?'

'Good thinking,' said Brett. 'We'll do that.'

Saying goodbye to the teacher, they descended to their left for a few yards, and then started to follow the contour round the hillside, going just east of north. Then the slope began to turn leftwards in a north-westerly direction. (Look at the map and you will see that they were at the head of the valley, on the pass between the big hill on the right and the two smaller hills on the left.) They could look down at the narrow valley which they were following on their orienteering course, and they could look over now to the valley on the other side of the hills, which was broader, with more gentle slopes.

The hillside turned south-westwards and they followed it for about half a mile before it began to straighten out and turn just north of west. Above them on the right the slopes continued up to the summit, and below them on the left they could see the brightly clad forms of Carol and Peter struggling up the hillside, which was rather steep at this point.

'You were right, Brett,' said Rebecca. 'Your route was best. We've overtaken them and they had a start on us.'

They continued on their contour, neither climbing nor descending, and very soon they reached the stream. It flowed gently downhill from the plateau and before long they came to the lake. Mr Wallis, the art teacher, was there, making a sketch of the landscape.

'Hello,' he said. 'So you've made it. Well done. Not much farther to go.' Like the other two teachers he made notes in a book while Brett and Rebecca consulted the map once again. They couldn't see far in the direction of the youth hostel, which was control number four, for the land in front of them sloped gently before dropping steeply, and then flattened out again in gentle slopes (wide contours, close contours, wide contours again).

'We'd better take a bearing,' said Brett. 'Once we reach the steep slopes we should be able to see the hostel if we're on the right course. If we can't see it, we can take a bearing on the north-eastern corner of this wood, "aiming-off" again, so we can follow the edge of the wood till we reach the hostel.'

Spreading the map on the ground, they placed the compass edge on the line of travel from the lake to the hostel. Then Brett turned the compass housing until the red orienteering lines were parallel with the grid lines. They read off the bearing – 240°; then they turned the compass housing anticlockwise to add 9° for the magnetic variation – the field bearing was 249°. They turned themselves round until the magnetic end of the compass needle pointed to the N on the rim of the housing and then started down the gentle slopes which faced them. Soon they came to the steeper slopes and right at the bottom saw a few fir trees. But the view was obstructed by a curious line of rocks; they couldn't see the hostel at all, nor the corner of the wood.

'What shall we do now?' wondered Rebecca.

'We'll just have to follow the bearing,' replied Brett. So down the hill they went, walking quickly. They reached the rocks – strange boulders bigger than buses, strewn around as if a careless giant had absent-mindedly dropped them.

'Aren't these strange?' said Rebecca. 'I wonder where they came from?'

'Perhaps they're the remains of a cliff that's worn away,' replied Brett. 'I don't really know, we'll have to ask Miss Dobson. But look, there are the trees and I think I can see the hostel.' He pointed at a grey speck against a dark background of fir trees.

'Yes, yes, yes!' whooped Rebecca. 'And we're dead on course, too!'

Miss Wells was outside the hostel and they chatted to her for a moment before looking up number five on the map – another stream junction. Brett suggested that Rebecca should lead them to the control point, the last one on the course. The stream junction was south-east of the hostel, about half a mile away and about forty feet farther downhill.

'Shall I take a compass bearing on the junction?' Rebecca asked herself. 'Oh, no, we might miss it, then we won't know whether to go up- or downstream to find the junction.' She was looking hard at the map, studying all the possibilities. 'We don't need a compass bearing,' she said. 'Look, Brett, if we contour eastwards on the level we are now, we'll hit the stream above the junction, then we only need go downstream to find it. That'll be OK, won't it?'

It was, and they set off along the hillside in a just south of south-east direction. The weird boulders were above them and the ground at their feet was covered with small stones which had broken off the rocks, but they caused no difficulty in walking. After about fifteen minutes they reached the stream, then turned southwards following it downhill. There was a yellow flag at the junction and Miss Brown was there.

'You've done well,' she said. 'You're the first ones to get here.' She wrote down their names and made a note of the time. 'You've completed the course, and I want you to go down to my house and wait there for everyone to get back. Miss Dobson's there too. Just follow the stream down to the road and my house is by the road bridge over the stream. Off you go, and well done!'

'Fancy being first back,' said Rebecca as they walked down along the stream. 'We've won, haven't we?'

'We don't know yet,' replied Brett. 'Sue and Robin left after us and they might complete the whole course in less time than we've taken. But we've certainly taken less time than Peter and Carol and Adam and Jane – they left before us and we overtook them.'

Later, when the whole group was assembled at Miss Brown's house and Miss Dobson had checked all the teachers' books, Brett and Rebecca were acclaimed as the winners. Their time was 2 hours 45 minutes, ten minutes faster than Sue and Robin who came second. The busload of children and teachers were tired and contented after their day on the hills. It had been a good day, a kind of treasure hunt using maps and compasses and their native wits. There was still a lot to learn about map-reading and navigation, but it was a good start.

If you read this story again, you will see that this is really an orienteering exercise. As a competition sport, you need the help of adults, but there is nothing to stop you from planning a route on the map as Brett and Rebecca did and following it yourself. Use 'handrails' as much as possible, as they did when they followed the powerlines. It is rather wearying travelling *all* the time on a compass bearing; you have to be very slow and cautious to avoid going off the bearing, so look out for things on the map that will help you: powerlines, streams, walls, a path, and so on. When taking a bearing, 'aim-off' if the object you want to locate can't easily be seen from the distance; a stream junction, for example. But if the object is a church tower there will be no problem. You can also use 'attack-points' if there is a large, easily seen object near the one you are making for, such as the corner of a forest. Take a bearing on the easily seen object and either follow the bearing or 'handrails' to it; then from here to the control you can take a very accurate compass bearing – over the short distance to travel there should be no difficulty in walking exactly on the bearing.

For further information

The British Orienteering Federation will give you any further information you would like, including what junior clubs there are in your area. The address is:
British Orienteering Federation,
National Office,
11 Balmoral Crescent,
West Molesey,
Surrey.

Some further books to read on orienteering and navigation are:
Map and Compass Way: Orienteering by John Disley, Blond Educational
Nature is your Guide by Harold Gatty, Collins
The Challenge of Orienteering by Gordon Pirie, Pelham Books
Orienteering ('Know the Game' Series), Educational Productions.

Crossword quiz 2

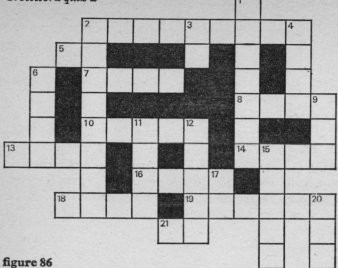

figure 86

Across

2 Compete in following map clues
5 Either
7 Streams run — 6
8 Opposite 18
10 Book of maps
13 Map of your house
14 Don't go any further
16 When you've opened a gate,
   — it again
18 Sun sets here
19 Eat me on a picnic
21 Public house
(See **Answers**)

Down

1 Measurements on a compass
2 Survey department of the
   Army
3 Not yes
4 Lines
6 Has steep slopes
9 The peak of a 6
11 Not the first
12 Not north
15 Runs on tracks
17 Towards
20 Grows in mixed wood

8 Going on a journey

When you are travelling by car, train or aeroplane, the best game
of all is to follow your journey on a map.

Road maps

A walker or a cyclist uses a 1-inch (1:50 000) or a 2½-inch (1:25 000)
map of the area he wants to explore, but a motorist needs a map on
a smaller scale. He travels so fast that he would need several 1-inch
maps for a single journey. A good road map has a scale of between
six and ten miles to the inch, or about 1 centimetre to 6 kilometres.
It will show towns, villages, railways, international and county
boundaries, airports, ferries and spot-heights.

It will also, of course, show roads! These will be colour-coded.
Motorways may be coloured in blue, other major trunk roads in
red, class B roads in another colour; and minor roads are shown in a
fine network of thin red lines. The map will have a key at the bottom
to show the colour code and other symbols used. The distance
between the towns may be shown on the roads in miles or kilometres.

The map might also show additional information of interest to the
motorist: places of historic interest, beauty spots and views. It may
also show relief in the form of layer-tinting (the scale is too small for
contours to be used).

Planning your route

When you are going on a long car journey it is a good idea to plan
your route first, using your road map. In this way you can bypass
crowded town centres. At important holiday times it is essential to
plan your route carefully if you want to avoid the delays caused by
heavy traffic on main roads. You can make the maximum use of
minor roads and sometimes travel through unexpectedly pretty

country while you may be only a few miles away from all the traffic which has ground to a halt in a cloud of petrol fumes on the main road!

The Ordnance Survey publish maps on a scale of four inches to the mile, which will before long be metricated, and these can be used as road maps if you are not travelling so far that you would go off the sheet. These maps use layer-tinting and contours to give an immediate impression of relief. Parks and forests are also shown. Even if you are not using one of these maps to plan your route, it is still useful to have in the car, for you can pick out places of interest that you are passing. By orientating the map you can identify mountains and hills. It will give you a lot of pleasure and interest as you sit in the back seat getting cramp in your bottom and possibly becoming bored with sitting still for so long.

After you have planned the route, you can summarize it in strip-map form, as shown in **figure 87**. Most drivers welcome a good navigator in the car because it is difficult to read the map and drive at the same

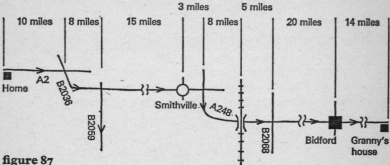

figure 87

time. So why don't you navigate next time you go out driving? Plan the route first, write it down as a strip map, then refer to it when you give the instructions – you'd better agree that this is what you are doing first! If you navigate well, you will be a welcome passenger in any car – and who knows, one day you may navigate in a Monte Carlo Rally.

Journey record

Keep a notebook for records of journeys which you make in the car. Your record sheets could be like this one, or there may be other information you wish to add.

Date								
Time of departure								
To								
From								
Distance as crow flies								
Mileage travelled								
Time of arrival								

Average speed   Points of special interest

Guessing distance

When you use maps it is very important to understand what the distances on the map mean when you are on the ground. Earlier in this book you measured miles and kilometres on foot. This game will help you to judge distance as you travel.

The players choose a landmark some distance ahead along the road, then guess how far away it is. The real distance can be checked on the car's mileometer.

How long is a mile?

The umpire gives the signal and the players shut their eyes and estimate how long it takes the car to travel a mile (or a kilometre if that is the measurement on your car), or two miles, or whatever distance you choose. As each player thinks that you have travelled the chosen distance, he calls out 'Now!' and opens his eyes. The one who guesses nearest according to the mileometer (either above or below) is the winner.

You can get very accurate at this estimating with practice. Of course, if everyone will guarantee not to peek at the mileometer, you can also play this game with your eyes open.

Country of origin

This game is best played over a period of time on various journeys. You will need an outline map of the world, which you can trace off an atlas map.

Each country has different letters to identify its cars when they travel abroad. (For instance, you can see the letters GB on the back of British cars which travel overseas.) See how many you can collect and mark on your map of the world.
Here are some of the identifying letters you are most likely to see:

A	Austria	GB	Great Britain
B	Belgium	I	Italy
CH	Switzerland	IRE	Ireland
D	Germany	N	Netherlands
E	Spain	S	Sweden
F	France	USA	United States of America

(You can find a more complete list in the AA or RAC handbook.)

County of origin

Each county in Britain also issues different letters for car licences, so you can tell from the licence plate where the car was registered. Lists of these index marks are given in the handbooks of the AA and the RAC. See if you can collect one car for each county. Record your score on an outline map of Britain. You will be surprised by how much this game improves your knowledge of the map of the country.

The map-symbol game

This game needs to be prepared before you start the journey. On a piece of white card mark down a number of Ordnance Survey symbols depicting objects that you might pass on a journey. The list in **figure 88** will give you some ideas.

This list is long and could be extended even further. Each symbol is given a points value. On an ordinary run through mainly urban and country areas, you will see many pubs, so we give public houses a low points value, say 1. But you will see few windmills and even fewer battle sites, so these will have correspondingly higher values. On a journey which is mainly along the coast, the coastal features (such as lighthouses, flat rocks and sandhills) will have lower values; and correspondingly higher values will be given to things like pubs, churches, telephone kiosks, and so on. Each player has a notebook and pencil and looks hard through the car window. Each object seen which corresponds with a symbol on the list is marked down, together with the score. At the end of the journey the scores are

		Suggested score values			Suggested score values
✝	Church with tower	4		Cliffs	10
✝	Church with spire	4		Flat rocks (on beach)	12
▲	Youth Hostel	5		Weir	12
	Bus station	8		Wood	6
	Quarry	9		Orchard	8
	Power lines (pylons)	5	——	Multiple track railway (main line)	5
	Windmill	15	------	Narrow gauge railway	10
	Glasshouses	10	P	Post Office	6
	Bridge over river (or canal)	5	PH	Public house	1
	Marsh	8	Castle +	Antiquity, or site of antiquity	15
	Sandhills	9	✕ 1066	Site of battle (with date)	15

figure 88

totted up and the winner, of course, is the one with the highest
score. This is a good exercise in observation – essential if you are to
become an intelligent navigator!

9 What else do maps tell us?

We have talked so far mainly about maps which help us to find our way. Now let's look at some maps which give us other sorts of information.

It is possible to draw maps which show such things as the history of an area, the population, the kinds of crops which are grown, the mineral and other natural resources, the climate. A map outline can be used to present a great deal of different information.

Compare these maps
Here we give you four maps of Australia to show you how the same basic outline map can have information drawn onto it to tell you

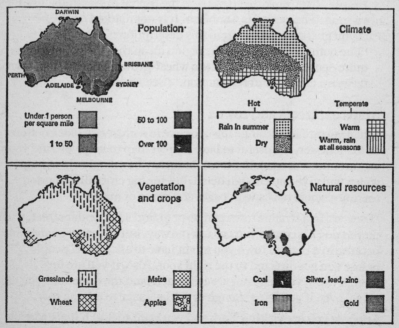

figure 89

different things. If you compare these maps you will be able to answer a number of questions about Australia.

1 Where do most people live in Australia – around the coast or in the interior ? Why do you think that this is so ?

2 What work do you think people around Brisbane may do ?

3 Where do Alice and Thomas and Jane and Mark live ?

a 'We have a funny combination of "crops" around our area,' says Alice, 'coal and apples!'

b 'We get a lot of rain in our summers,' says Thomas. 'It helps us to keep the grass on the grazing lands growing for the sheep and cattle.'

c 'The Gold Rush opened up my city,' says Jane. 'We have a good climate which helps to make it a popular area for many people to live.'

d 'Way out in the west where I live, it's often very hot and we're not far from the near-desert lands, but my uncle grows wheat very successfully,' says Mark.

4 People often think that Sydney is the capital of Australia, but they are wrong. The capital is Canberra. It is not marked on the map. Can you guess where it is from this description:

'The natural resources in the region mean that the population is quite dense for Australia. It is a wheat-growing region, too, with its warm climate and regular rain.' (See **Answers**)

Maps of streets and towns

When you are in a strange town, or live in a great city like London or Manchester, it's useful to have a street map to help you find your way around. For a smaller town there may be a single-sheet map which will give you enough detail, but for big cities like London there are whole books with pages and pages of maps.

If you are in a strange town and want to find a particular street, what do you do ? Of course you can ask the way, but that may be difficult because in a biggish town you might have to ask several people before you got directed to the right spot. Also, if you are in a foreign town, you may not always understand the directions you are given, even if you have enough of the language to ask the way.

Suppose you are visiting York and you want to find King's Manor.

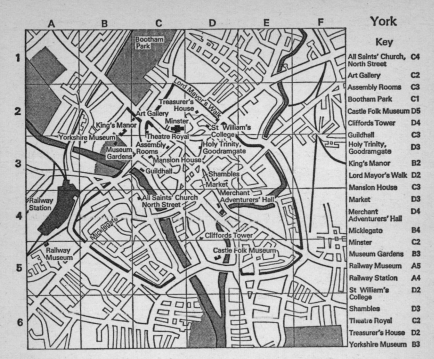

figure 90

What would you do ? Somewhere on the street map of York there
would be an index or list of all the street names in the city. Assuming
you know the order of the alphabet, you look up the name in the
list. In **figure 90** the *key* gives part of the index for the centre of
York.

After each street or place name there is a number and a letter. Now
look at the map excerpt. You can see that it has a grid on it and that
along the top of the map there are letters, while down the side there
are numbers, so that each square on the map has a reference number
and letter. To find a place on the map you use exactly the same
method as for finding a grid reference. Let's take the first name on
the index, All Saints' Church. The index tells us that it's in square
C4, so we locate the row of squares under C. We then find the row
of squares numbered 4 and then scan both rows of squares. The
point where the two rows meet is square C4 and the church is in the

105

top left-hand part of the square. Have you found it ? Now see if you can find all the other places in the list in the same way.

When you are looking at a map book, like the one for London or for Birmingham, the list in the back of the book has two numbers and a letter. The first number gives the page on which the street is shown; and the second number and the letter tell you the square in which the street is.

But you can tell more about a town from a map than just where you can find different streets. You can see where there are open spaces like parks and football grounds, you can see the railway lines, and in the case of a city like York, you can see the ancient city walls, the churches and the cathedral, and other places of special interest like the market place and the museums.

History through maps

By comparing maps which are made at different times, you can see how a town has grown because, in Britain at least, there are very few towns which have grown to their present size and shape in as short a time as a century. Even a new town or suburb may change its shape over a period of ten or twenty years.

We show here in a series of imaginary maps how the town of Greenshoots has changed over the centuries. Many of the very old buildings, like the church, are still there today. Around them, new buildings, both public and private ones, have grown up. Some buildings have disappeared or their use has changed. If you compare the maps in **figure 91** you will see how the town has grown, and been altered and extended.

The development of your town

You can make a very interesting map to show how your own area has developed over the years and what materials were used in the construction of the buildings.

When you start you can use fairly wide divisions of time, but later, if you become really interested in your researches, you can go into more detail. If you live on an estate which was built more or less all at one time and mostly in the same style, then you may need to go into a neighbouring area for your study.

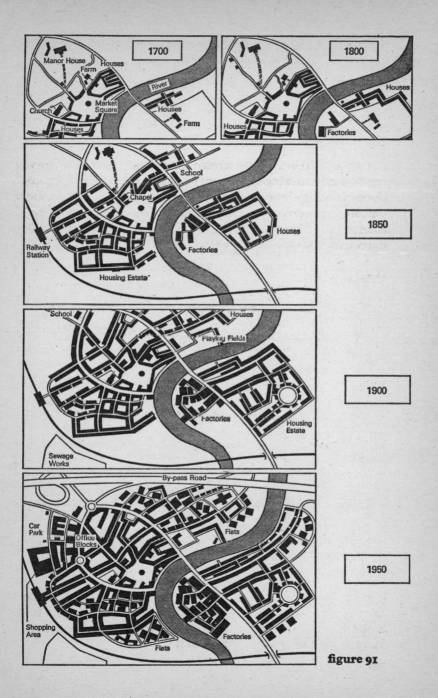

figure 91

The period divisions you might use are:

sixteenth century
seventeenth century
eighteenth century
nineteenth century and up to 1918
inter-war period (1918–1939)
post-war (since 1945)

When you are collecting information for this sort of study your map-board (see page 48) will be very useful to you. You will need a map of the area you are studying and you may also need sheets of paper to take down any extra information you collect.

Try to find out as much as you can with as little help as possible from people outside your family, but once you have begun to build up a picture of the area, do ask people politely if they are willing to help you.

Here are some rules for getting help from other people:
1 Introduce yourself
2 Explain what it is you are doing
3 Show the work you have done so far
4 Then, if you get an interested and willing response, ask your questions.

The sort of things you might want to ask are: 'Do you know when your house or shop was built?' 'Do you know how old the church is?' 'Can you remember when the village hall was built?'

Some of the most common building materials you will find are: brick, pebble-dash, timber, stone and stucco. You can write this information alongside your dates on the map and you will build up a picture of how building materials have changed over the centuries.

Street names

In days past, trades were often carried on in particular areas or streets of a town. See if you can find street names in your town which recall old trades or activities which were carried on in them. Look for names like Baker's Lane, Weaver Street, Market Street and so on. Can you find other street names which recall the past? Can you find out more about these trades?

Other street names recall the period at which they were built. Bloemfontein Avenue and Springbok Road were probably built at the beginning of the century at the time of the South African Boer War. Some streets were named after the former use of the land on which they were built: Windmill Road, Grain Farm Avenue and so on. In London you find many street names which recall the old streams and rivers which now run underneath the streets of London: Ladbroke Grove (broke = brook), Fleet Street (the Fleet River), and Westbourne Grove ('bourne' being an old word for 'stream').

One-way streets

If you live in or near an area which has a system of one-way streets it is interesting to make a map of the system showing how it works. As you are probably usually a pedestrian this system may not have concerned you much. If you were a driver it would! See if you can decide what was the planner's purpose in devising this particular system. Was it to keep traffic away from residential areas? Was it to avoid traffic jams at junctions? Are the streets too narrow for two-way traffic? Can you think of any other reasons?

What happens in these buildings?

Another interesting map can be made to show how buildings in your area are used. This sort of map can be made in a High Street or town centre rather than in a housing area where all the buildings have much the same use. If, however, you live in a village, you will find that different users may well all be mixed up, as in this typical village street.

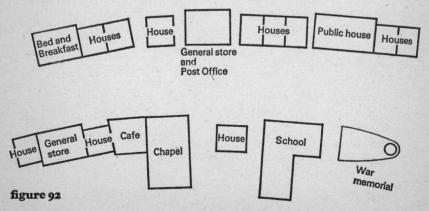

figure 92

If your map shows the use of buildings in a High Street, you might also like to look at the use of the upper storeys of the buildings. Usually you can discover this by looking at the sign boards at the entrance. Sometimes you will have to ask people. Be sure to be very polite and explain the purpose of your questions. The postman is the person who may be able to help you most.

Here is a map showing the use of a row of buildings in a small local shopping centre in central London.

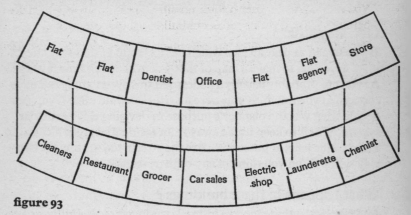

figure 93

Maps of open spaces

We have talked so far about maps which show buildings. People are more and more concerned about open space, both for recreation and just so that built-up areas don't spread into every corner, leaving nowhere for wild flowers and animals. Of course, if you live in the country you may find this hard to understand, but if you live in a big city, you will find it only too easy!

Do you know where the open spaces are in your area ? Can you record them on a map of the locality ? But open spaces are not all of one kind. Some are public open spaces like parks and playing fields; some are private like orchards; some come into neither category, either because they are 'wild' land or because they are 'lost' land (like the centres of roundabouts or vacant plots of land which are not being used for building or any other purpose).

So you will need a key to your map to show the different uses of the open spaces. The key below might be suitable for your purposes or you can devise one of your own:

Playing fields, parks   yellow ☐

Market gardens, nurseries, orchards   red   ☐

Woods, heath and other wild land   green ☐

'Lost' land   brown ☐

You might add another colour, possibly grey, for areas which are being used but are not yet lost to buildings, like car parks.

Perhaps you could add some specimens of dried wild flowers, leaves and grasses to your map to show what wild life you have actually found in the open spaces.

A map of farm crops

If you live in (or often visit) the country, you could make a map showing the uses of the land and buildings on a farm. If you need help from the farmer or farm workers, don't ask them when they are busy. Perhaps you could arrange to visit them in the evening or in their meal breaks.

A farm map could be decorated with pictures of what the various crops which are grown on the farm actually look like, as well as showing the uses of the farm buildings. You will be able to map the shape of the fields by referring to an ordnance survey map.

Links with the world

If you feel confident about asking people for information, you might like to try finding out and illustrating on a map the links which some houses in your locality have with the outside world.

It's a good idea to start with your own family. Here are some of the questions you could ask:

1 Where do the children go to school?
2 Where do the grown-ups work?
3 Where does the family do most of its ordinary shopping?
4 Where do they buy big things like furniture and clothes?
5 What local paper do they read and where is it published?
6 Where do they go to the cinema/doctor/bank?

If you have collected material from, say, four houses in your street, your map illustrating this information might look like this:

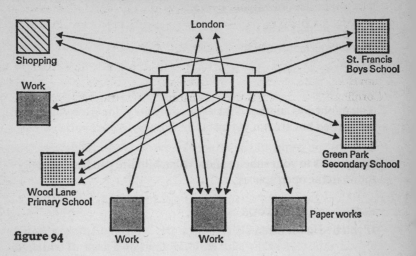

figure 94

Where did the contents of your larder come from?
Here is a good mapmaking game for a rainy day when you can't get out. You will need a biggish outline map of the world on which you can identify at least the larger countries. Trace one out of an atlas. Now look at all the tins and packets in your larder (make sure you put them back in the right order later!) Try to find out from the labels or from your own knowledge where the contents originated. Record this on your outline map either in words or in symbols.

A quick look in my larder revealed the following:

Rice from southern USA	Corn from Canada
Sugar from Barbados	Coffee from West Africa
Spaghetti from Italy	Tinned tomatoes from Italy
Tea from India	Ravioli from France
Sardines from Spain	Pie-filling from California, USA
Tuna fish from Japan	Chestnut purée from France
Soya sauce from Hong Kong	Bananas from Jamaica
Oranges from Israel	Apples from Australia

Often food is packed in Britain and you will have to do a bit of research to find where the contents are likely to have originated.

You can go on to develop another map which shows you where the food came from in Britain. Make another map of Britain and mark on it the places where the food was processed and packed. See how far these foods had to travel to fill your larder.

A spot-check in my larder revealed the following:

Sugar from London   Crispbread from Poole, Dorset
Jam from Manchester   Mustard from Norwich
Cornflour from Esher, Surrey   Peanut butter from Derbyshire

10 More ways to use your map-reading skills

Some useful organizations

The Guide and Scout Associations

Ask at the public library or your school for the address of your local
association. The idea behind the Scouts and Guides is to train
young people (from eleven to sixteen years) to look after themselves
and other people. They hold regular meetings and have other
weekend sessions and camps. They learn to use maps, how to deal
with emergencies, how to interpret the weather, and generally how
to survive outdoors.

Youth Hostels Association

Trevelyan House, St Albans, Herts.

The Scottish Youth Hostels Association

7 Glebe Crescent, Stirling, Scotland.

The Youth Hostels Association runs a large number of hostels all
over the country which provide a cheap and simple base where
people who want to explore the countryside can stay. Anyone can
join the YHA from the age of five years, but until you are twelve
years old you must go with your parents or someone over eighteen
years old. The YHA Handbook, which you will receive when you
join, gives you a lot of useful information about how to plan a trip
using hostels and about the sort of equipment you will need.

You can use the hostels for both holidays and shorter trips at
weekends. Many hostels have a great number of regular weekend
activities in which you can join and so add to your experience of
using a map on the ground.

The YHA also runs a number of organized holidays which offer
special training in a variety of subjects from mountaineering to
pony-trekking and from canoeing to bird-watching.

The British Mountaineering Council

26 Park Crescent, London W1.

The Council will put you in touch with your nearest mountaineering club, where you will be able to receive training and gain experience in mountaineering activities. It also publishes a number of booklets on the subject.

The Council advises that 'map-reading is an essential skill for any mountaineer or any person who visits mountains for any purpose.'

The Cyclists Touring Club

Cotterell House, 69 Meadrow, Godalming, Surrey.

Through the Cyclists Touring Club you can get lots of advice about cycling: route planning and good places for cycle touring as well as practical advice about the care and equipment of your bicycle. The CTC has 200 local clubs where you can meet other people with similar interests and take part in a variety of activities: competitions, rallies, organized tours in Britain and abroad.

British Orienteering Federation

We have given details of the work of this organization in the chapter on orienteering, page 94.

Duke of Edinburgh's Award Scheme

2 Old Queen Street, London W1.

The scheme is concerned with the individual achievements of young people from fourteen years upwards. The Bronze Award covers four main areas: service to the community, interests or hobbies, physical activity for boys or 'design for living' for girls, and an expedition. Mapmaking can be one of the hobby subjects, but of course it is for the two-day walking or cycling expedition that map knowledge is essential for all entrants. These expeditions must have a planned purpose, such as visiting places of interest and discovering useful information. You must go through a period of preparation before you undertake such an expedition and part of this training is, of course, map-reading and the use of a compass. If you are interested, you can write for further details to the scheme's office.

How to become a professional mapmaker

If you become really interested in maps and mapmaking, you may like to know about two careers where you could work and use your interest. One is that of a cartographer; the other that of a surveyor of land or of water.

The surveyor does the measuring of roads, buildings, hills, valleys and other features, and records them in their correct positions so that the cartographer can revise maps such as the Ordnance Survey map, and keep them up to date.

Most cartographers work for the government but they may also be employed (usually on a freelance arrangement – that is, working at home and being paid for the work done) by publishers and by tourist organizations to make maps for books, travel pamphlets and guides. Think of all the travel books, the atlases, the school textbooks and tourist guides which have maps. Many of these maps, particularly the more detailed ones, are drawn by cartographers.

To train as a cartographer you will need passes in the General Certificate of Education (GCE) Ordinary ('O') Level or Grade One Certificate of Education (CSE) in two or three of the following subjects: English language, mathematics, geography, art, technical drawing, a modern language or surveying. Jobs are advertised in the newspapers, but your Youth Employment Officer should be able to advise you about where to apply. You are then trained on the job, rather like an apprenticeship.

There are two sorts of surveyors: land surveyors who measure the physical features of town and country, and hydrographic surveyors who measure and record information about seas, rivers, tides, currents and other water features. (*Hydro* means water and 'graphic' refers to things which are drawn or written.) Most of these surveyors work for the government, but some work for oil companies and in other offices.

You can start to train as a surveyor at the age of sixteen if you have five GCE 'O'-Level or equivalent passes. These must include English language and mathematics. To take higher qualifications you will also need two passes at GCE Advanced Level.
There are three methods of training. You can work as a paid trainee

for four to five years and study part-time through correspondence courses or at a technical college for your examinations. You can take a three-year degree course in civil engineering, mathematics, physical science or geography and follow this with a postgraduate course in land surveying. You can take a CNAA (Council of National Academic Awards) degree in surveying. You cannot take your final surveying examinations until you have had four years' experience in land or hydrographic surveying.

If you would like more detailed information than this, write to:
The Royal Institution of Chartered Surveyors
12 Great George Street, London SW1.

The Ordnance Survey Department
Chessington, Surrey.

Admiralty Hydrographic Department
Whitehall, London SW1.

Map quiz

Now that you have read this book and tried out many of the games and activities described in it, you will have learned quite a lot about maps. See how many of these questions you can answer without looking back.

1 How much (approximately) is 48 kilometres in miles?
2 How much (approximately) is 105 miles in kilometres?
3 What is the map symbol for
   (a) a telephone (b) a church (c) a marsh (d) a station?
4 What do these symbols mean? (a) 🔺 (b) P (c) 🗺️
5 How can you use your watch to find direction?
6 What is the Country Code?
7 What are the do's and don'ts for mountain climbers?
8 What is a plain scale?
9 How would you measure the length on a map of a winding country path?
10 What is a contour line?
11 What is meant by gradient?
12 What is a key on a map?
13 What are the cardinal points of a compass?
14 What is a large-scale map?
15 What is meant by Representative Fraction?
16 Where does the sun rise, and where does it set?
17 How could you find north at night?
18 What is magnetic north?
19 What is an easting?
20 How do you take a compass bearing?
21 How would you find your position on a map?
22 What is orienteering?
23 How do you walk on a compass bearing?
24 What is layer-tinting?

The answers are on page 126.

Answers

Here are the answers to the questions and puzzles in the text.

page 11

page 14

A = 2
B = 1

page 18

From Rebecca's house to the school is 175 metres.
From Mark's house to the shop is 150 metres.
From the shop to the bus stop is 40 metres.
From Adam's house to Mark's house is 270 metres.
The school playground is about 50 × 50 metres – 250 square metres in area.

page 22

1 $2\frac{3}{4}$ miles
2 $3\frac{1}{2}$ miles
3 $2\frac{7}{8}$ miles

page 23

The rose bed is 44 feet long.
The garden hut is 5×7 feet.
The path is 60 feet long.
The area of the lawn is 42×60 feet.

page 26

1 windmill
2 church
3 woods (deciduous, coniferous, mixed)
4 marsh
5 main road
6 minor road
7 footpath
8 branch-line railway joining main-line
9 main-line and branch-line railway stations
10 minor road going over bridge
11 youth hostel
12 public house

page 42

A5, B3, C1, D4, E2.

page 43

1C, 2E, 3D, 4B, 5A.

page 56

They were wise to avoid the stream when they were lost because streams have a habit of taking short cuts down mountains – which often means the steepest, rockiest routes.

page 58

Number 2 is the correctly orientated map.

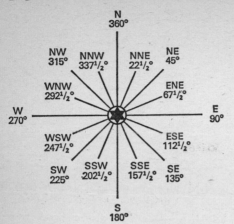

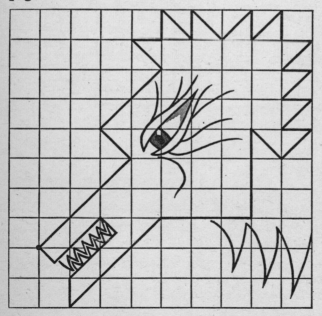

page 74

1. public house at 6647
2. post office at 7347
3. orchard around 3555
4. bridge at 5536
5. church at 7852
6. steep slope at 4388
7. castle at 5688
8. bus stop at 8534
9. river from 1073 to 6710
10. ferry at 6317

page 81

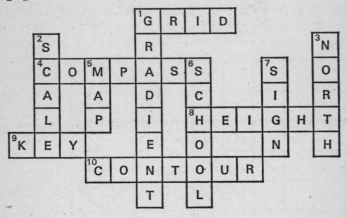

page 95

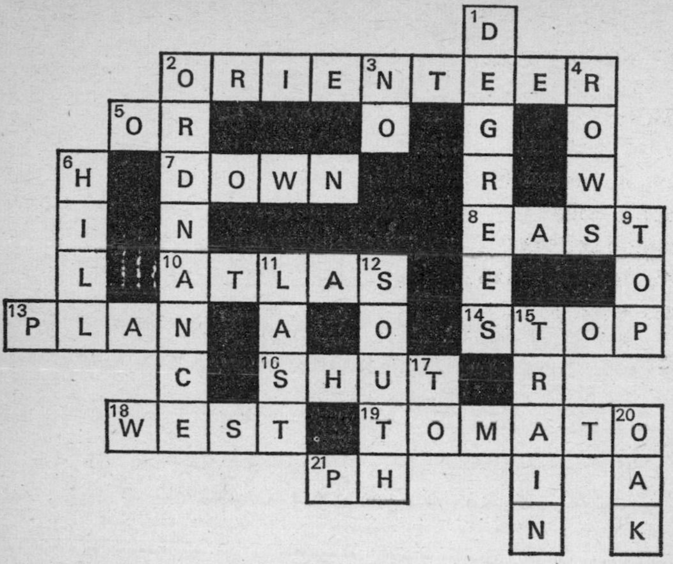
D
ORIENTEER
OR O G O
H DOWN R W
I N EAST
L ATLAS E O
PLAN A O STOP
C SHUT R
WEST TOMATO
PH I A
N K

page 104

1 Around the coast, because the climate is better than in the very dry interior; the main natural resources are also near the coast.
2 Wheat-farming
3 (a) Sydney (b) Darwin (c) Melbourne (d) Perth
4 Canberra is about 100 miles south and slightly west of Sydney.

Answers to Map Quiz on page 119

1 30 miles.
2 168 kilometres.
3 (a)   (b)   or   (c)

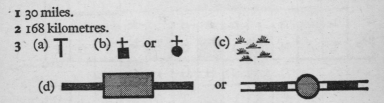

(d)   or

4 (a) youth hostel (b) post office (c) mixed wood.
5 Refer back to pages 65–6 if you don't remember.
6 Refer back to page 49.
7 Refer back to the Mountain Safety Code on page 50.
8 Refer back to page 17.
9 Refer back to page 22.
10 An imaginary line joining all points of equal height.
11 The steepness of ground, expressed as a 1-foot rise (or fall) in
    a distance of so many feet.
12 The key gives an explanation of all the symbols used and of the
    information given on the map.
13 North, south, east, west.
14 Large-scale maps show a small area in great detail; small-scale
    maps cover a much greater area, but show little detail.
15 Refer back to page 20.
16 East and west respectively.
17 From the Pole Star. Refer back to pages 64–5.
18 Refer back to pages 66–7.
19 Refer back to page 72.
20 Refer back to pages 75–8.
21 Refer back to page 59.
22 A competitive sport of finding one's way around the countryside
    using maps and compasses to locate points by means of grid
    references.

23 Best way is to fix on intermediate points exactly on the line of your bearing (see pages 68–70). Refer back to page 69 for method of skirting round obstacles.

24 Refer back to page 36.

Deborah Manley and Diane James
Piccolo Craft Book 50p

Here is your chance to find out how to make all kinds of lovely things, using a whole range of materials and techniques.

Deborah Manley, Peta Ree and Margaret Murphy
Piccolo Holiday Book 40p

Holidays are times to do things, learn things – and have fun! Here are a whole lot of ideas, from making a weather chart to doing your family tree or forming a secret society.

Anthony Greenbank
Survival for Young People 45p

Anyone, any time, can be faced with an emergency, indoors or out. If a fire traps you in a room, someone is drowning or you are lost in unknown territory, would you know what to do? Read this book and you will be prepared for most of them.

Climbing for Young People 60p

Anthony Greenbank gives a step-by-step course in climbing for everyone who wants to learn to climb easily, sensibly and above all, safely. He takes you through your first experiments with boulders and simple, practical training schemes that you can carry out at home, to dry runs in lowland areas and finally to your first real climb.

You can buy these and other Piccolo books from booksellers and newsagents; or direct from the following address:
Pan Books, Sales Office, Cavaye Place, London SW10 9PG
Send purchase price plus 20p for the first book and 10p for each additional book, to allow for postage and packing
Prices quoted are applicable in UK
While every effort is made to keep prices low, it is sometimes necessary to increase prices at short notice. Pan Books reserve the right to show on covers new retail prices which may differ from those advertised in the text or elsewhere